# JESUS
## THE MEDIATOR

WILLIAM L. BROWNSBERGER

# JESUS THE MEDIATOR

THE CATHOLIC UNIVERSITY
OF AMERICA PRESS
WASHINGTON, D.C.

For Francesca, Joseph,

Marcello, Mariella, Francesca,

and William


The paper used in this publication meets the minimum requirements of American National Standards for Information Science—Permanence of Paper for Printed Library Materials, ANSI Z39.48-1984.
∞

Library of Congress Cataloging-in-Publication Data
Brownsberger, William L.
Jesus the mediator / William L. Brownsberger.
p. cm.
Includes bibliographical references and index.
ISBN 978-0-8132-2119-9 (cloth : alk. paper) 1. Jesus Christ—Person and offices. 2. Jesus Christ—Mediation. 3. Mediation between God and man—Christianity. I. Title.
BT255.B76 2013
232'.8—dc23 2012040529

# CONTENTS

# INTRODUCTION

The Gospel of John ends with an acclamation that should serve as a warning to anyone who wishes to offer a contribution to the field of Christology: "There are many other things that Jesus did and, if each one were written, I suppose that even the world could not hold the books written." John's point, which applies immediately but not exclusively to Christ's instruction and *magnalia,* was reinforced by the eventual rejection of Tatian's *Diatesseron,* which sought to harmonize—and thereby reduce—the story of Jesus into a single perspective. No human expression[1] can of itself represent the Person and mission of Jesus Christ in an adequate way; every Christology is beset by limitations in its vantage point. These limitations are quite evident in the present work. It will be immediately clear that this book is not a comprehensive study of Christ. Its breadth is limited to a very few questions and I intend the reflections in it

1. Cf. *Dei verbum,* 13.

to complement, rather than necessarily to compete with, other insights into the character and mission of the Lord.

In this short book I propose several theses—some classical, others not so classical—toward an understanding of Jesus as Mediator. All of these theses gravitate in some degree around the question of Jesus' identity and psychological faculties—intellect, will, and affectivity—in their connection to salvation. I do not, however, propose to elaborate a soteriology in the strict sense; I rather wish to say something about the Incarnate Person that soteriology must presuppose. More specifically, the way that the Word suffers and acts *humanly* as Mediator will be the subject of the following reflections.[2]

This book's first chapter adumbrates an understanding of the human knowledge and self-consciousness of Christ. Today these two issues must be approached from within a larger context than has often formed the parameters of and motivations for their discussion in the past. In this chapter we already begin to see the importance of that which we suppose in soteriology: the larger context required is readily available in the kerygmatic fact of salvation. In the best in Christian thought kerygma has consistently defined the edges of theological explanation, while theology in turn has informed and clarified proclamation. In the present case, I argue that the fact of salvation itself is dynamically oriented toward an account of the psychological reality of the one who has accomplished this fact; taking salvation as a given, we seek its underlying conditions, or *Bedingun-*

2. Much could be said, of course, about specifically divine mediatory activity; however, as we will see, this is Trinitarian and as such cannot be brought into direct focus in the space of this study.

*gen der Möglichkeit,* in the Person and human features of Jesus.[3] An account of this kind that focuses on Christ's knowledge and consciousness is of particular importance since salvation is itself a relationship to the Savior and relationships, in the best sense, involve some form of understanding of the other. To understand, on a theological level, the Person to whom human persons are related as saved, we are faced with the task of coming to terms with (rather than dismissing) a somewhat technical and far-ranging discussion that was carried out in the continental theology that immediately preceded the Second Vatican Council. Although the language that characterized this discussion has fallen into disuse and the problematics addressed by its participants will seem antiquated, my hope is that the first chapter will suggest that there is something in these debates that is indispensible to a fully developed Christology. That there may be truth in this claim is supported by the fact that a handful of scholars—whose work I also wish to incorporate here—has kept the central concerns of these debates alive, even if issues are engaged in different terms. The fact, however, that the issues that will concern us in the first chapter have not enjoyed a widespread and sustained interest in post-Conciliar theology accounts for a somewhat uneven weighting of immediately pre-Conciliar formulations and explanations.

The second chapter also represents a return of sorts. The thought of Maurice Blondel provided a strong source of inspiration for a Catholic theology that sought to "perfect

3. Since I take salvation and the personal and psychological structure of Christ to be mutually illuminating, I will at other points proceed in the opposite direction, namely, from Christ's personal and psychological structure to a fuller understanding of salvation.

and augment," in the apt phrase of Leo XIII, that edifice of which the neo-Thomist revival had been the lone custodian. Blondel, like his neo-Thomist counterparts, played a key role in opposing the compromise settlement (which is hardly ever a true settlement) between the Church and the modern world that was Modernism. Blondel's role in this endeavor was often misrepresented or underestimated; indeed, he was for a time conflated with the Modernists whom he opposed. Yet, as his correspondence with Alfred Loisy attests, he forcefully opposed the Christological reductionism to which Modernism had committed itself and he did so in philosophical terms that had not been dismissed virtually a priori by his opponents. Perhaps, as some have noted, it is the echo of Berkeley's *Esse est percipi* that resounds in Blondel's assertion that the human knowledge of Christ is instrumental in reality's constitution and, correspondingly, in mankind's salvation. Since the second chapter is primarily occupied with Christ's understanding, it serves to round out the theses put forward in chapter 1. In this chapter, however, we begin to move from the consideration of Christ's intellect to that of his other human faculties.

In the third chapter, we turn to the human will of Christ in its role in uniting finitude and infinity. G. W. F. Hegel sought to correct a commonplace notion of infinity with an articulation of it that was at once more pure and more powerful. Theology in the twentieth century exploited this notion with some measure of success in its doctrine of God, but Christology itself was left relatively untouched by the reformulation. Even if Hegel's understanding of the infinite is not to be accepted uncritically, it is provocative of a deeper appreciation of

Christ's volitional life and his exercise of virtue in connection with redemption. In focusing on salvation, by extending the theme of Christ's embodiment of virtue to human practice, this chapter plays the role of chiastic center in our reflections.

Chapter 4 complements the discussion of infinity begun in the preceding chapter by asking whether there is finite being in Christ united to the infinite Being of his Person. St. Thomas introduced the notion of an *Esse secundarium* in Christ in a disputed question toward the end of his life. This formulation nuances, but does not disavow, Thomas's earlier insistence that Christ has one *Esse simpliciter*. Not only is Thomas's reformulated position more defensible theologically and philosophically, it also seems to open up insights into the matter of salvific mediation. That Christ not only unites finitude and infinity in his voluntary life, as suggested in chapter 3, but is himself the union of finitude and infinity will have consequences for our understanding of soteriology.

While the fifth chapter seems at first glance to be something of a stand-alone, since it is not clearly paired with another chapter, it should be taken in connection with everything that precedes it. No psychological portrait of Christ as Savior would be sufficient, even in the merest sense, without some investigation of his emotions. Accordingly, we resume our descent through the traditional taxonomy of Christ's faculties—which is somewhat interrupted by chapter 4—with a look at his sensitive life. Anger, alone of the emotions, is treated here as representative of and as connected to the full spectrum of human feeling. I will seek to show that not only is Jesus not sinful in his anger, his anger is itself salvific. This final theme returns us to the soteriological consideration that begins and governs the book.

Not everyone will find himself or herself in sympathy with the orientation of this book. Some readers will find themselves little in sympathy with the answers that I proffer; for others, the questions themselves that I ask should not be entertained in their present form or even at all. I recently came across a work that begins by warning away prospective readers who would be likely to feel cheated upon finishing the text. I have no wish to be off-putting, but I think that it is only fair to extend the same caveat here. Readers who have arrived at the conviction that classical theology and philosophy have little to offer to contemporary Christology should probably invest their time elsewhere. On the other hand, readers who think that St. Thomas can have no truck with Hegel, Blondel, or the French in general are bound to find themselves bewildered and frustrated by this work's approach. With proper esteem for narrative, existential, and poetic modes of discourse in theology, I believe that a direct and assertorial style is also both warranted and desirable. I believe that theological statements have a practical and pastoral import, but that such statements do not depend on the ready discernment of this feature in them as a criterion for their validity. I believe that remarkable and extraordinary things are not necessarily untrue things. I also believe that all true things must be true together. I will have more to say shortly about my starting points, but I hope that putting these few cards on the table straightaway will forestall grief and save time.

I appreciate and am grateful for the reader's investment of time and energy. This book is a short row to hoe, but the field of Christology is full of hard clods.

# JESUS
THE MEDIATOR

[ 1 ]

# CHRIST'S HUMAN CONSCIOUSNESS

Held with an equal steadfastness, all of the elements of Christological and Trinitarian dogma keep the mind of the theologian in a tension that is at once crucifying and extraordinarily fecund. By disallowing every narrowing and constriction, all reduction of Mystery, this tension opens the way to a deepening of understanding.[1]

1. Translations throughout are mine unless otherwise indicated. "Tenus avec une égale fermeté, tous les éléments du dogme trinitaire et christologique maintiennent l'intelligence du théologien dans une tension crucifiante, mais extraordinairement féconde. En empêchant tout rétrécissement tout écrasement, toute réduction du Mystère, cette tension ouvre la voie à l'approfondissement et à la recherche"; see M. J. Le Guillou, preface to François-Marie Léthel, *Théologie de l'agonie du Christ: La liberté humaine du Fils de Dieu et son importance sotériologique mises en lumière par Saint Maxime Confesseur,* Théologie Historique, vol. 52 (Paris: Éditions Beauchesne, 1979), 6. For a similar sentiment, see also Helmut Riedlinger, *Geschichtlichkeit und Vollendung des Wissens Christi, Quaestiones Disputatae,* 32 (Freiburg, Basel, and Vienna: Herder, 1966), 9: "Wer es wagt, nach dem Wissen Christi zu

## PRELIMINARY REMARKS

The vantage point of soteriology, as I have just mentioned, has constantly provided insight into Christological questions. The Cappadocians provide a vivid example of profiting from this perspective in the fourth century, but theirs is by no means unique in the history of Christian theology. Informed by this historical lesson, theology should investigate the knowledge and consciousness of Christ under the aspect of soteriology.[2] A relatively unprofitable course in investigating the psychology of Christ, even after the great codification of Christological doctrine accomplished by the seventh century, is to grant first that there is a God-man, two natures and one Person, and to wonder next how much this Person can know in his human intellect. In following this deceptively straightforward approach, the reconciliation of our understanding of the God-man with our notion of his mission would be an afterthought at best. In contrast, we must observe a rather strict connection between ontology and soteriology.[3] This does not mean that doctrinal

fragen, muß sich zunächst in einem weiten Fragefeld umsehen und inmitten der Vielen, die hier miteinander und gegeneinander fragen, den rechten Weg suchen."

2. For a dim view on the advisability of undertaking this endeavor, see Ivor Davidson, "'Not My Will but Yours Be Done': The Ontological Dynamics of Incarnational Intention," International Journal of Systematic Theology 7, no. 2 (2005): 178–204, 200: "Any attempt to construct a 'psychology' of Jesus—and the quest appears to hold lingering attractions in various quarters, generating an ongoing literature both critical and devotional—is in no small measure doomed to failure, and may be in peril of yet more serious evils." For contrast, cf. Vincenzo Battaglia, O.F.M., "I 'Sentimenti' del Signore Gesù: Un modello cristologico per la vita spirituale e l'agire morale," *Antonianum* 81 (2006): 209–55, 245–46.

3. Cf. Yves Congar, O.P., "Pour une Christologie pneumatologique: Note bibliographique," *Revue des sciences philosophiques et théologiques* 63, no. 3 (1979): 435–42, 435–36. Cf. also François-Marie Léthel, *Théologie de l'agonie,* 109–12, on

contributions to the subject of the constitution of Christ are not guiding principles throughout; still less does it mean that we are free to disregard them and reinvent the Incarnate Word according to a fluid and subjective interpretation of Scripture. It does, however, signal the importance of the Incarnation in our understanding of the Word. He became man "*for* us men and for our salvation." The questions of who he is and how he is constituted cannot be separated from those of what he does and why he does it.

A "low" Christology, which tends to downplay the extent and depth of Christ's understanding, may observe this point quite naturally and unselfconsciously. Accentuation of the Word's self-emptying, or *kenosis,* emphasizes Jesus' sharing the human lot and redeeming humanity through this solidarity; redemption is tightly linked to hominization. Without gainsaying anything in the true doctrine of *kenosis,* the possibility

---

the (harmonious) relationship of history and ontology regarding Christ. On 111, Léthel says: "[E]n affirmant … l'ontologie du mystère, on ne nie pas du tout l'histoire du mystère: au contraire, on la fonde théologiquement comme histoire de salut." Cf. further Christian Duquoc, *Christologie: Essai dogmatique* (Paris: Les Éditions du Cerf, 1972), 145. Also on this theme 149–54 et passim indicates a danger in doing theology from Scholastic maxims while ignoring the Bible and gives examples of theologians who avoided this route. Throughout the chapter "Le Christ prophète" runs the theme of relating Christology to mission and not to an ontological principle of perfection. In connection with the link between soteriology and Christology, Wolfhart Pannenberg's caution is worth keeping in mind; see Wolfhart Pannenberg, *Jesus—God and Man,* 2nd ed., trans. Lewis L. Wilkins and Duane A. Priebe (Philadelphia: Westminster Press, 1977), 38: "[T]he divinity of Jesus does not consist in his saving significance for us. Divinity and saving significance are interrelated as distinct things. The divinity of Jesus remains the *presupposition* for his saving significance for us and, conversely, the saving significance of his divinity is the reason why we take *interest* in the question of his divinity." See also 47–49. On Pannenberg's view, see further D. R. de Lacey, "Jesus as Mediator," *Journal for the Study of the New Testament* 29 (1987): 101–21, 103.

that I would like to explore is that of how soteriological concerns fit easily with—or, perhaps, even require—a Christology that focuses on the perfections of Christ, including that of his human mind. This type of investigation, of course, is not new, but it has lost nothing of its relevance in the wake of recent Christological discussions. As we proceed, then, let us bear in mind that it will not suffice today to stand on the principle, however true, that we cannot attribute too many perfections to Christ: *De Christo nunquam satis.*[4]

I should be clear from the beginning about what I do not intend to do in investigating the soteriological import of Christ's knowledge and consciousness, so as not to create expectations

4. It hardly needs to be said that a theologian's beginning with Christ's mission does not necessarily lead to a high Christology. See, e.g., Alexandre Durand, "La Science du Christ," *Nouvelle Revue Théologique* 71 (1949): 497–503, 498: he signals that in the nineteenth century theologians began to replace the deductive psychology of Christ that starts in his absolute perfection with a psychology based on his relative perfection, that is, one that considers first his mission as Redeemer. A relevant question emerges in the wake of this: Is not the concern to present Christ as full of knowledge based on an excessive valuation of knowledge itself, seen quantitatively and as an end in itself? On 502–3 Durand says that nothing is taken away from Christ if he does not know this or that—Jesus is perfect in his own order. He argues that limited knowledge is part of his exinanition. For a contemporary argument in favor of high Christology, specifically Christ's possession of the beatific vision, that very deliberately avoids invoking the principle of maximal perfection, see Thomas Joseph White, O.P., "The Voluntary Action of the Earthly Christ and the Necessity of the Beatific Vision," *The Thomist* 69 (2005): 497–534, esp. 515. For White, Christ's human volitional life depends for its authentically filial character on his knowing directly (and not by faith) the will of his Father. (The attempt to expand the notion of faith prevalent in late antiquity and through the Scholastic period and to argue in favor of Christ's possession of faith is represented by Hans Urs von Balthasar, *Spouse of the Word,* vol. 2 of *Explorations in Theology* [San Francisco: Ignatius Press, 1991], 43–79 and by Gilles Mongeau, S.J., "The Human and Divine Knowing of the Incarnate Word," *Josephinum Journal of Theology* 12 [2005]: 30–42, 32–34.) Guy Mansini, O.S.B., "Understanding St. Thomas on Christ's Immediate Knowledge of God," *The Thomist* 59, no. 1 (1995): 91–124, 96–98, shows that St. Thomas does not rely on the principle of perfection.

where I have no pretenses. I do not intend to settle the biblical-exegetical question about the knowledge of Christ. Jesus' apparent ignorance of the coming Day of Judgment (Mt 24:36, Mk 13:32) and the Lucan declaration that Jesus grew in wisdom (2:40, 2.52), among other texts that seem at first blush to suggest limited knowledge in Christ, have served as standard test cases in this question from its patristic reception down to its contemporary treatments. I do not believe that a "maximalist" Christology is at variance with the plain sense of Scripture, as I hope to show by a few examples, but the immediate aim of the present discussion precludes my arguing the exegetical point at length.[5] More will be said about this subject anon, but suffice it to mention at present that the paucity of biblical references in the pages that follow does not reflect on my part any marginalization of Scripture's importance in general or in its relevance to the present task; it rather reflects my belief that we are in no position to understand that which the Bible may say about Jesus' thinking without clearing the air on some very fundamental issues first. No one wishing to investigate the exegetical dimension to this discussion, in any case, will lack available reading.

Similarly, I will not attempt an assessment of the relevant texts from the Catholic Magisterial tradition or argue at length for a particular evaluation of doctrinal and disciplinary pronouncements. Nonetheless, I intend to present a picture of Christ's psychology that concords with Magisterial treatments of this question and will have occasion to mention a few significant declarations in the course of this study.

5. Cf. *Lamentabili*, 32.

We do not have the opportunity here for proper exegesis or a close analysis of Magisterial pronouncements, yet our task here will be to hold together the basic Christian ideas concerning Christ and his mission, biblical and traditional, and to do this without sacrificing any one element to defend any other.[6] Certainly unavoidable will be the impression of having highlighted some elements while having left out others; the figure of Jesus is so dense and complex that each reader of the Gospels will have his or her own portrait of Jesus in mind. While I cannot forestall such an impression, I can attempt to mitigate it by being candid from the beginning about the basic Christian ideas that I have in mind: Jesus is one, divine Person with an integral, assumed, human nature through which God has saved the human race. While it may seem that I am being flippantly terse in laying out the ideas that I wish to explore, I proffer that they provide more than enough to

6. Davidson would see the aspiration of holding everything together as subject to great risk, to say the least. See Davidson, "Not My Will," 185: "The perennial temptation is to attempt to adjust one side or the other in order to depict a person who is, as it were, psychologically credible—to trim, for example, aspects of what divinity might mean in order to fit the parameters of humanity, or to submerge the reality of Jesus' human struggles in the depths of a divine agency that renders his moral dedication as a human subject somewhat less impressive that it otherwise appears to be. On the one side, divine willing is scaled down to the proportions of human choosing, in all its precariousness and structural infirmity; on the other, human willing is only ostensibly authentic, since divinity remains in direct hegemonic control. To take the first route is to jeopardize the full force of the New Testament's insistence that Jesus' actions are expressive of an utterly firm, albeit utterly gratuitous, divine purpose—that the Son comes into the world to fulfill a will that originates in God's own heart and is outworked according to God's invincible determination, with effects that humanity on its own could not achieve. To take the second path is to risk the falsification of Jesus' human choices and decisions, to suggest that he is either subject to forces beyond his control or even coerced into acting in ways strongly contrary to his own desires."

deal with here, especially since we cannot shrug off the task of holding in harmony everything that these concise statements imply.

### CHRIST AS HUMANLY SELF-CONSCIOUS

Although soteriological considerations determine the shape of our discussion, we cannot simply begin with an account of redemption.[7] The Scholastic maxim holds true here: the first in

7. Several excellent summaries of the points in controversy in the following are available. I do not attempt to put together a comprehensive picture here of the debates and casts of characters involved in the Christological controversy of the mid-twentieth century (or of any other time); I intend to reference issues and thinkers principally as needed to make specific points. In addition to works specifically referenced elsewhere in this chapter, special mention must be made of the following. Marco Cé, "La Discussione sulla coscienza umana di Cristo nella teologia moderna," *La Scuola Cattolica* 80 (1952): 265–303, gives a spirited, defensive summary of Galtier and a clear overview of Parente's thought. Pages 267–73 are valuable for the nineteenth-century roots of the problem of Christ's human consciousness, which include some interesting anticipations of the twentieth-century form of the question. Additional historical background can be found in Luigi Jammarrone (also spelled "Iammarrone" in the literature), O.F.M. Conv., *L'Unità psicologica in Cristo,* Selecta Seraphica, vol. 1 (Rome: Editrice "Miscellanea Francescana", 1962), 4–15, 23–68, offers a good summary of the Catholics of the twentieth century. Christian Duquoc, *Christologie,* 322–24 provides a helpful summary of Deodat de Basly, Seiller, and Galtier, while 324–28 recapitulates the thoughts of Galot and Rahner. Jean Galot, S.J., "La psychologie du Christ," *Nouvelle Revue Théologique* 80, no. 4 (1958): 337–58, is invaluable for an overview. Paul Galtier, "La conscience humaine du Christ," *Gregorianum* 35, no. 2 (1954): 225–46, illuminates his own perspective on the issues in controversy. Jean-Jacques Latour, "Imago Dei invisibilis: Esquisses sur les relations de l'anthropologie chrétienne et de la psychologie du Christ," in *Problèmes actuels de christologie,* ed. Humbert Bouëssé and Jean-Jacques Latour, Textes et études théologiques (Bruges: Desclée De Brouwer, 1965), 227–34, is very helpful for seeing how the different theological assumptions held by key players in this controversy impact answers to Christological questions. Raymond Maloney, S.J., *The Knowledge of Christ,* Problems in Theology (London and New York: Continuum, 1999), 88–89, lists theologians who accept, in one way or another, the traditional ideas of Christ's extraordinary knowledge, those who do not, and those who take a middle position in this area. Jacques Dupuis, S.J., *Who Do You Say I Am? Introduction to Christology* (Maryknoll, N.Y.: Orbis Books,

the order of intention is the last in the order of execution. We must start by assembling key features in the picture of Christ's human nature, rooted in his divine Person, from the material of Christian belief. In this way we will arrive at the soteriology that has been latent in and determinative of our discussion all along. By means of discussing Christ's knowledge and intentionality, we can "back into" the truth that, if the most heroic human actions are deliberate, so also must be Christ's self-sacrifice. Let us begin, then, with a thought that is somewhat disputed today: Christ's foundational human act is knowing God immediately.[8]

---

1994), 114–16, also provides a useful and succinct overview, as does Pannenberg, *Jesus—God and Man,* 328–31. Several valuable bibliographies are dedicated to the present set of questions; two of the most helpful have been Engelbert Gutwenger, S.J., "The Problem of Christ's Knowledge," in *Who Is Jesus of Nazareth?* trans. Theodore Westow, Concilium, vol. 11 (New York and Glen Rock, N.J.: Paulist Press, 1965), 97–98, and Karl Rahner, "Dogmatic Reflections on the Knowledge and Self-Consciousness of Christ," in *Theological Investigations*, vol. 5 (Baltimore: Helicon Press, 1966), 193–94 and 196–98. In addition, Angelo Amato, *Gesù il signore: Saggio di cristologia,* 3rd ed. (Bologna: Edizioni Dehoniane Bologna, 1993), 415–17, also offers an excellent bibliography.

8. Charles-Vincent Héris, "Problème de christologie: La Conscience de Jésus," *Esprit et Vie* 81 (1971): 672–79, 676, refers to the fact that that Galot denies that Christ had the beatific vision and that Galot dismisses the 1918 Holy Office and *Mystici corporis* statements as disciplinary and outdated. Christian Duquoc, in *Christologie,* 160, also makes the argument that the 1918 statements from the Holy Office are disciplinary, regarding teaching, rather than doctrinal, as does Jacques Dupuis, S.J., *Who Do You Say I Am?* 121–22, which extends this appraisal to Pius XII's *Mystici corporis* as well. For a similar view of Magisterial interventions on this point, see also Jean-Pierre Torrell, "S. Thomas d'Aquin et la science du Christ: Une relecture des questions 9–12 de la 'Tertia Pars' de la Somme de Théologie," in *Saint Thomas au XXe siècle: Colloque du centenaire de la "Revue thomiste" (1893–1992), Toulouse, 25–28 mars 1993,* ed. Serge-Thomas Bonino, O.P. (Paris: Éditions Saint-Paul, 1994), 402, 409. Cf. Helmut Riedlinger, *Geschichtlichkeit,* 82. Cf. also Terry J. Tekippe, "Towards a Systematic Understanding of the Vision in Christ," *Method: Journal of Lonergan Studies* 11 (1993): 77–101, 84: "[T]he status of this doctrine [Christ's possession of the beatific vision on earth] may be judged to be authori-

Christ's reception of the beatific vision is the basic and fundamental condition of his consciousness, although the vision is not consciousness itself.[9] Christ's posterior human reflection

tatively but not infallibly pronounced." Tekippe's article is worthwhile reading on this subject. Noteworthy is his capable treatment, on pages 85–101, of four common objections to Christ's enjoyment of beatitude on earth: that which sees vision in competition with freedom, with suffering, with learning, and with humanity. Engelbert Gutwenger, in "Christ's Knowledge," 92, avers that Christ's having had the beatific vision during his life on earth is difficult to reconcile with his freedom. For different perspectives on some issues presented in these pages, including the claim that Christ had the beatific vision on earth, see also John McDermott, S.J., "How Did Jesus Know He Was God? The Ontological Psychology of Mark 10:17–22," *Irish Theological Quarterly* 74, no. 3 (2009): 272–97.

9. See, e.g., Natalino Spaccapelo, S.J., "La coscienza di Cristo," *Science et Esprit* 26, no. 1 (1974): 5–37, 10, 14–15, 19–20, and 26: objective knowledge of Christ's divine identity is not consciousness itself. See, in contrast, the interesting reference to theologians who say that the beatific vision, by reason of its experiential and immediate character, can be identified with consciousness in Cé, "Discussione," 300. Cf. Galot, "Psychologie," 349: Galot argues that the beatific vision can only provide knowledge, not consciousness. Also in agreement is Galtier, "Conscience humaine," 226: seeing the beatific vision cannot be identified with consciousness. Later, for example, at 231, he speaks of the beatific vision as providing the *knowledge* that the divine Person underlies the human intellect. Interesting in this connection is also Jammarrone, *L'Unità psicologica,* 258–65 et passim: the beatific vision is not consciousness. The subject and object are neither identical nor immanent to each other. Thus, there is no way to talk about a true human consciousness of the Word. (We will explore this issue later.) Cf. Bernard Lonergan, S.J., *The Ontological and Psychological Constitution of Christ,* trans. Michael G. Shields, in the *Collected Words of Bernard Lonergan,* vol. 7 (Toronto, Buffalo, N.Y., and London: University of Toronto Press, 2002), 212–13. Christ attains his Self as subject—not under the formality of the intelligible (objective knowledge) but under the formality of the experienced. He is like us in all things but sin and "nos attingimus inquantum conscie sentimus." Cf. Lonergan's compact formulation in Frederick E. Crowe, ed., *A Third Collection: Papers by Bernard J. F. Lonergan, S.J.* (New York, Mahwah, N.J., and London: Paulist Press and Geoffrey Chapman, 1985), 91: "Man's sensitive, intellectual, rational, and moral operations have two distinct but related characteristics. They are both intentional and conscious. Insofar as they are intentional, they make objects present to us. Insofar as they are conscious, they make us present to ourselves." For a treatment of Lonergan's and Rahner's contrasting understandings of consciousness and knowledge, see Raymond Maloney, S.J., "The Mind of Christ in Transcendental Theology: Rahner, Lonergan and Crowe," *Heythrop Journal* 25 (1984): 288–300, esp. 288–91.

on the beatific vision replicates in time and in the created order the eternal divine self-presence of the Word. In this reflection, Christ as man confirms the I that is eternally founded. Within the vision of the Trinity, Jesus humanly identifies himself as the Son of the Father.[10] Two related claims are at issue here and we must keep them distinct in order to unite them. On the one hand, we must say that Jesus is related to the Father; indeed, his personal identity is precisely in procession from the Father. Although we certainly would want to say much about *what* Jesus is, the question of *who* Jesus is can be answered with the simple statement that he is *from the Father.*[11] On the other hand, without prejudice to texts such as Mt 11:27, Jn 3:31–32, 8:26–27, 15:15, and so on, which refer to the Son's knowledge of the Father, when we affirm that Jesus had the beatific vision, we mean that he humanly knows the whole Trinity in an immediate way. Jesus' human self-understanding, which is achieved in the beatific but which is not identical to the beatific vision, is the creaturely crystallization of his eternal, personal identity in relationship to his Father.[12] Notwithstanding the fact that his humanity (*what*) is a creature of the Triune God, the identity

10. On Jesus' filial humanity, see Juan Alfaro, S.J., "Person and Grace," in *Man Before God: Readings in Theology,* ed. Juan Alfaro and Denis Burkhard (New York: P. J. Kenedy & Sons, 1966), 188–192, and Dupuis, *Who Do You Say I Am?* esp.126–27. See also White, "Voluntary Action," 498–99, 522–24, et passim, which aptly expresses the human crystallization of Christ's eternal, personal relation to the Father.

11. Even his co-originating relation to the Spirit, albeit bound up with his identity, flows from this.

12. Cf. Thomas G. Weinandy, O.F.M., Cap., "Jesus' Filial Vision of the Father," *Pro Ecclesia* 13, no. 2 (2004): 189–201, 193–94, et passim. For a contrasting view, see Philipp Kaiser, *Das Wissen Jesu Christi in der lateinischen (westlichen) Theologie,* Eichstätter Studien, vol. 14 (Regensburg, Germany: Verlag Friedrich Pustet, 1981), 294–300.

of the Second Person of the Trinity (*who*)—even *in* his humanity—is tied to the Father.[13]

If the humanity of Christ is instrumental in salvation, in a way that we will discuss shortly, we must understand that this human instrument is filial in the Person of the Son to which it belongs; in a relational (not creational) sense, it is from the Father. Jesus can humanly speak and do nothing but what he hears from his Father.[14] In his humanity, the Son does nothing apart from his relatedness to the Father.

As man, he is the Father's Son. He fully establishes his identity as a man in becoming humanly aware of his divine and filial identity because, without awareness of self, humanity is not fully actualized. Thus, the beatitude around which this reflection centers is his first and grounding human operation. That to which he leads human persons is his from the first as his basic, orienting lodestar; humanly self-defined in the light of divine happiness, he is *simul viator et comprehensor.* St. Thomas argues that Christ can give that which he already has.[15] That which Christ has, he has in the primordial depths of his human experience and, more, as ontologically constitutive. There is no fissure between his mission and his identity.

Our consideration of Christ's objective understanding of his identity has not yet yielded anything specific about his

13. See Alfaro, "Person and Grace," 189: "[W]e must not forget that the divine person of the Word, which subsists in the humanity of Christ, is nothing other than the consubstantial terminus of the Father's eternal generation: it is the subsistent relation of divine sonship. The man Christ is a person only because he is the Son of God; this relation of the Word to the Father, and this relation alone, constitutes Christ as a person.... The Incarnation means that the man Jesus has the Son's relation to the Father, and that precisely this relation constitutes him as a person."

14. See, e.g., Jn 5:30.

15. *Summa theologiae* (hereafter *ST*) 3, 9, 2.

consciousness. How is his human consciousness or his experience of self-awareness achieved over against the beatific vision? Human subjectivity is established in act.[16] In, but as distinct from, acts of objective knowing and willing the human person is—in the language of Transcendental Thomism—coknown, that is, known obliquely and not thematically. Such subjective experience is regularly objectified in subsequent reflection; it is by so doing that the person comes to embrace his or her identity. The first fully human act—in which the actor is coknown and by which he or she knows himself or herself—is achieved for human persons in light of material experience—*Nihil in intellectu quod non prius in sensu* (nothing is in the intellect that was not first in the senses).[17] Christ, in contrast, humanly coknows himself in knowing the refulgence of divine glory. His primordial subjective intellectual experience is correlative to an act of understanding that is, in contrast to common human acts of understanding, both nonsensory and nonconceptual. Yet, for all of the differences between the content and mode of this knowing and of our own, Christ truly possesses objective knowledge in this vision. He must also, as all human beings do, turn toward himself in objective knowledge. Thus, two moments of objective knowledge—the beatific vision itself and Jesus' objectifying reflection on his own subjective experience—join in Christ's self-understanding. It would be strange to suggest that when he turns toward him-

16. Cf. *ST* 1, 87, 1 and 3.

17. See, e.g., René Le Troquer, P.S.S., *What Is Man?* trans. Eric Earnshaw Smith, Twentieth Century Encyclopedia of Catholicism, vol. 3 (New York: Hawthorn Books, 1961), 31, and Karl Rahner, S.J., "The Body in the Order of Salvation," in *Theological Investigations,* vol. 17 (New York: Crossroad, 1981), 71–89.

self in objective knowing he does not bring in intentionality that which he attains in the beatific vision (a "secondary object"[18] of which is the Incarnation). Jesus understands himself as humanly knowing God and as God humanly knowing. Yet this consideration does not clear away a fundamental question for us: Do we have to say that the beatific vision is necessary for self-knowledge? If, hypothetically, it were absent—and Christ were only conscious in conceptual human knowing—would he know himself humanly as God?[19] Perhaps in raising this question at all we are trying to derive too much from consciousness: Is consciousness some sort of apprehension of essence or is it of the existence of a subject only?[20]

A look at the question of Christ's human knowing and consciousness in connection with the beatific vision as these issues were debated in the middle decades of the twentieth century will help us to clarify this issue and, further, to see its implications for the psychology of Christ.

18. The so-called primary object of the beatific vision is classically understood as God himself, one and three. Secondary objects are contingent and created things, actions, events, etc.

19. According to the line of reasoning presented in Claude Sarassin, *Plein de grâce et de vérité: Théologie de l'âme du Christ selon Saint Thomas d'Aquin* (Venasque, France: Éditions du Carmel, 1992), esp. 32–35 and 38–44, the answer to this question can only be in the negative. Sarassin argues that God (only) knows himself directly, that is, without the mediation of concepts. Inasmuch as no human knowing, including that of Christ, is perfectly self-reflexive in this sense, natural human knowledge of divine identity is impossible. Christ only knows his identity in the supernatural grace of the beatific vision.

20. Jacques Maritain, *On the Grace and Humanity of Jesus* (New York: Herder & Herder, 1969), 114–15, argues that when Thomas talks about consciousness, he is not talking about attaining one's own essence—this is impossible—but about attaining the existence of the subject. Consciousness, which is a modern problem that Thomas never discusses explicitly, is experiential and perceptive—rooted in reflection on acts—and does not attain the essence of the soul.

## THEOLOGY AND THE QUESTION OF CHRIST'S HUMAN KNOWING AND CONSCIOUSNESS

We have just seen that the objective encounter with truth founds and conditions human subjectivity. In this context, we have tried to come to terms with how this logic of human knowing must play out in the case of Jesus' human intellect, which is in the presence of First Truth itself. At this point the question arises of in what sense the beatific vision is constitutive of Christ's self-awareness. Is it a sine qua non condition for his understanding his identity? For Paul Galtier, Christ's human knowledge of his divinity relies absolutely on the beatific vision; of itself alone, his human understanding cannot reach this. Galtier writes:

> Between [the Word] ... and the activities of his human nature, there had to be a link that would ensure his unity in the psychological order as the hypostatic union did in the ontological order. This link is the beatific vision, which was alone capable of establishing this unity, whence it follows that the presence of this vision in Christ can be said to belong to the order of his constitution.[21]

Christ's human intelligence has always known that Christ is also God, but it could not have acquired this knowledge of itself. Again, Galtier says: "Due to the beatific vision and to this only, the Word, in his human intellect, always knew him-

21. "Entre lui [le Verbe] ... et les activités de sa nature humaine, une liaison a dû exister qui assure son unité dans l'ordre psychologique comme le fait l'union hypostatique dans l'ordre ontologique. Cette liaison, c'est la vision béatifique qui, seule peut l'établir et de là vient que sa présence dans le Christ peut être considérée comme appartenant à l'ordre de sa constitution"; see Galtier, "Conscience humaine," 227.

self as incarnate. Without this, that intellect would never have perceived this mystery."[22]

22. "Grâce à elle [la vision béatifique] et à elle seulement, le Verbe, par son intelligence humaine, s'est toujours vu incarné. A son défaut, cette intelligence n'aurait pas perçu ce mystère"; see Galtier, "Conscience humaine," 231. We must distinguish Christ's having always humanly seen himself as God and man from a consciousness thereof—see Jammarrone, *L'Unità psicologica*, 39; for Galtier, Christ has knowledge (*conoscenza*) that his humanity subsists in the Word, but not consciousness (*coscienza*). See also 31–32. Cf. Angelo Perego, S.J., "Sull'Unità psicologica di Cristo: In margine ad un notevole studio recente," *Ephemerides Carmeliticae* 12 (1961): 105–15, 110: "[A]ppena l'intelletto creato del Salvatore è attuato dal lume della gloria, l'"Io' del Verbo … non è più termine sproporzionato per l'atto *conscienziale* del medesimo intelletto." The question of in what degree and sense Christ can in principle be humanly aware of his divine hypostasis has been the subject of serious enquiry. Jammarone believes that, while the divine Person as such transcends Christ's human consciousness (*coscienza*), he can humanly perceive his ontological constitution and his divine personality; see Jammarrone, *L'Unità psicologica*, 270 et passim. On the idea that the Person as the full possession of the divine Nature transcends Christ's human consciousness, cf. Maloney, *Knowledge of Christ,* 100, which summarizes Lonergan: "The 'ego' which appears in Christ's human consciousness may in fact be identical with a divine person, but the fact that it is divine is precisely that, *a fact,* which can be known only as the object of judgement. Hence our Lord's awareness of his own nature as a divine nature is not exactly a matter of consciousness, in Lonergan's narrow sense of that term, but is a result of a combination of consciousness and of Christ's direct vision of the divinity. Through human consciousness one might, as in the case of Christ, be conscious of a divine person, but not of the divine nature, since it was a divine person who became incarnate, not a divine nature. To imply such a consciousness of the divine nature, as Rahner seems to do, is to indulge in an undue mingling of the natures." For Jammarrone, the perception of hypostatic dependence that he gains is by means of his acts; see Jammarrone, *L'Unità psicologica*, 229–31 et passim. The fuller understanding of the Incarnation, which escapes his human knowing, is supplied by the beatific vision; see 272–73, 295–96, et passim. Cf. Cé, "Discussione," 278: for Galtier, human awareness does not terminate in a person; its activity is the perception of acts as attributable to a nature (as is true of all humans). Whether that nature subsists in itself or in another person is outside of its scope. Luigi Jammarrone, in *L'Unità psicologica,* 109–17 et passim, raises and treats the question of whether consciousness terminates in nature or in person. See 297 and 140–44 for a good summary of his position here: consciousness terminates in a person, where person and nature coincide simply (as in us) or in a sense of hypostatic dependence in the case of Christ. By divine intervention, the human consciousness of Christ can clearly terminate in his Person without mediation by acts; there is direct

Galtier's declaration that the human understanding of Christ cannot reach Christ's identity leaves Galtier open to the charge that Christ's human intelligence would be in error. Dom Herman Diepen, for example, argues that if Jesus' human acts are perceived as acts of the human nature only, then Christ's human awareness (*conscience*) is fundamentally false and the beatific vision is indispensably corrective. On this reckoning, the beatific vision would show that the acts actually belong to a different subject—and not to the human nature, as supposed. This is a false solution, thinks Diepen, to the imaginary problem created by the view (to which we will return later) that nature is a real subject.[23] Instead, Diepen argues, we have to say that the Incarnate Word, by his human intelligence, perceives his human acts to be acts of *someone* and not of his human nature. The divine Person is outside of the purview of the human awareness (*conscience*) itself, but aided by the beatific vision Christ can humanly perceive a supernatural object. Thus, by human consciousness alone, Christ perceives his human acts to be dependent acts—not autonomous acts; it is not necessary that he sees by his human intellect the *someone* behind the acts. This *someone* is supplied by the beatific vision which completes—not corrects—the open-ended human understanding of his acts.[24] Galtier, for his part, pro-

self-perception (or personal perception) in grace. Cf. Latour, "Imago Dei invisibilis," 235–36: consciousness, understood as nonobjective, terminates in a person.

23. We will be to see this point from a better perspective further on, after we can looked at the fundamental issue of person and nature.

24. Herman Diepen, O.S.B., *La Théologie de L'Emmanuel: Les Lignes maîtresses d'une Christologie* (Bruges: Desclée de Brouwer, 1960), 189–90. Cf. 217, which recapitulates these ideas and adds to them that Christ humanly realizes the lack of a human I and already suspects the existence of the divine I, which the "intuitive vision"

tests that according to his view rightly understood, the beatific vision does not correct any error. Even though Christ's human intelligence cannot alone attain his identity, the information that it does gather is incomplete rather than false. The beatific vision completes, rather than redresses, the knowledge (*connaissance*) of Christ.[25]

Other authors also reserve a crucial place for the beatific

---

shows to him plainly. Cf. the criticism of Diepen on this point in Maritain, *Grace and Humanity,* 116, note 72.

25. Galtier, "Conscience humaine," 232–33. On 225 Galtier can also quote Réginald Garrigou-Lagrange to the effect that awareness of Jesus' divine personality comes from the beatific vision. For Garrigou-Lagrange's further articulation of this point, see Réginald Garrigou-Lagrange, O.P., "L'unique personnalité du Christ," *Angelicum* 29 (1952): 60–75, 70–71. For Garrigou-Lagrange, without the beatific vision Jesus would have been "conscious" of his divine personality—not as divine or uncreated—but as it would have borne or governed the deeds and undertakings of a human ontological person (which is obviously lacking in this case). Cf. Luigi (Aloysius) Ciappi, "De unitate Ontologica ac Psychologica Personae Christi," *Angelicum* 29 (1952): 182–89, 188–89: Christ does not have human consciousness of his suppositum; he humanly understands the unity of his Person by means of the beatific vision only. Charles-Vincent Héris, in "A propos d'un article sur la psychologie du Christ," *Revue des sciences philosophiques et théologiques* 43, no. 3 (1959): 462–71, 464, agrees with Galtier that the human consciousness cannot perceive the Person in itself. On 468, Héris raises the question of how Christ's human consciousness could come to the awareness of divine personhood, since it can only reach a human I? While the problem is the same in Héris and Galtier, their solutions differ. Héris shifts the source of Christ's awareness from the beatific vision (in Galtier) to infused knowledge; see 469–71. Héris, in "Problème de christologie," 675, again points to the fact that by itself, the human intellect cannot attain the divine personality. Metaphysical personhood would not make itself felt on the psychological level. Cf. also Roch Kereszty, O. Cist., "Psychological Subject and Consciousness in Christ," *Communio* 11, no. 3 (1984): 258–77, 265: Christ's human consciousness includes the direct awareness of his being the Son of the Father, which understanding substitutes for others' use of the notion of beatific vision (or else infused knowledge) in this connection. For more on the idea of Jesus' personal relation to the Father as it is employed here, see 272–77. Also interesting in regard to this general question are the reflections on 266–67. I also note at this point that I grateful to Fr. Roch Kereszty for his insightful comments on an early draft of this book.

vision in the question of Christ's thought. For Palemon Glorieux it is the way that he humanly knows himself to be God. He says of Christ and the beatific vision: "It is there that he perceives, in full clarity, the singular grace that he [God] has given him and where he knows himself to be the Son of God, where he sees his own mystery."[26] Karl Adam, as well, thinks along the same lines. He writes:

> If Jesus knew that his identity was divine, he can have attained this knowledge only through an especial, free act of Grace on the part of the triune God, only because the triune God opened Jesus' human consciousness at its zenith to the direct contemplation of his divine personality, and thus elevated his human consciousness into the sense of identity of the Logos. Since all that Jesus' humanity received from the Logos was only the divine identity and person, but no knowledge of this identity, and since on the other hand such a knowledge of his divine identity would be indispensable and absolutely necessary to him, we can only conclude that when the triune God endowed him with the incarnation, he also gave him the knowledge of this incarnation as soon as his human consciousness was sufficiently mature to understand the union.[27]

It is difficult fully to gauge the range of opinions on this issue.[28] We can say at least, however, that very often the beatific

26. "C'est là qu'il perçoit en pleine clarté la grâce unique qui lui [Dieu] a été faite et qu'il se sait Fils de Dieu, qu'il voit son propre mystère"; see Palemon Glorieux, "La révélation du Pére," *Mélanges de science religieuse* 42, no. 1 (1985): 21–41, 36.

27. Karl Adam, *The Christ of Faith: The Christology of the Church,* trans. Joyce Crick (New York: Pantheon Books, 1957), 267.

28. Cé, "Discussione," 300: Cé says that as far as he knows only Pietro Parente thinks Jesus humanly has direct conscious access to his divinity. All others think that Jesus receives knowledge of his divine personality from the beatific vision. (Page 291 describes Parente's notion that the Word is immediately attained in human consciousness as the coprinciple of Christ's actions.) Cf. Gutwenger's appraisal of opinion in Gutwenger, "Christ's Knowledge," 96: "There is only consent [among

vision is taken to supply information by which Christ humanly understands his divinity. Objective reflection on a coknown subject in Christ's human acts is widely taken to be insufficient of itself for producing in him an articulated sense of identity.

This question can seem somewhat speculative and idle, but one key place where it makes its soteriological importance felt is in the question of Christ's redemptive suffering. Marco Cé here signals a problem for us: If consciousness does not perceive the Word as the subject of suffering, can we say that the Word really suffered?[29] Of course, Christ can only suffer according to his humanity.[30] Yet—to further Cé's argument—if the suffering that Christ endures as a man is not in some way and measure consciously (as opposed to assertorially) connected to his Person, then paradoxically this human suffering would be without self-awareness—Christ would be suffering in something like the analogous way that animals are said to suffer and not as a man.

---

Thomists] on one point, and this is an important one: according to Thomistic teaching there is an immediate experience of the metaphysical personality in the human consciousness, a point of view that holds good also in christology and with which one can but agree."

29. Cé, "Discussione," 279. Cf. Jammarrone, *L'Unità psicologica*: "Aver coscienza di soffrire significa *percepirsi* come soggetto della sofferenza." Cf. Bernard Lonergan, S.J., "Christ as Subject: A Reply," in *Collection: Papers by Bernard Lonergan,* ed. F. E. Crowe, S.J. (New York: Herder & Herder, 1967), 192–94.

30. Cf. R. Haubst, "Welche Ich spricht Christus?" *Trierer theologische Zeitschrift* 66 (1957): 1–20, 12–13. On page 13, he says: "Daß ... das göttlich-hypostatische Ich nicht die psychologische Funktion eines schmerzerleidenden Ichs übernehmen kann, bedarf keiner weiteren Erörterung." In order to forestall Nestorian implications, Peter Geach draws attention to the importance of seeing the Second Person of the Trinity as the simple subject term of statements regarding his action (rather than, e.g., the compound Christ-as-man); see Peter Geach, *Providence and Evil: The Stanton Lectures, 1971–1972* (London, New York, and Melbourne: Cambridge University Press, 1977).

## PSYCHOLOGICAL IMPLICATIONS

The simple fact of suffering, however, is not yet a properly soteriological consideration. When we specify, as we just have, that we are dealing with suffering of a divine Person, who in his created nature both truly suffers and is truly self-aware in the way that other human being are, we find that we are at least on the trail toward our goal. If Christ has two integral and unconfused natures, then his divine "consciousness" remains distinct from his human consciousness. As a condition for this, we must say that Christ thinks in two real, integral intellects. This seems plain enough, but do we have any way of coming to terms with this idea or of determining it further? Even allowing for—or especially because of—the heavily analogical sense in which we apply "thought" or "intellect" to God and to human reality, we find that the way is hard going.

In articulating a conception of double thought, which corresponds to two unconfused, unmixed intellects, we are faced with two options. Either the intellects think two distinct and separate thoughts at any given time—they are on two tracks, as it were—or they think one and the same thought.[31] The for-

31. For an interesting contrast, see the view in Tim Bayne, "The Inclusion Model of the Incarnation: Problems and Prospects," *Religious Studies* 37, no. 2 (2001): 125–41, esp. 138–39. On 138, we read: "RI [Restricted Inclusionism] holds that at any one point in time Christ had only a single stream of consciousness. RI endorses what I called the *consecutive* model of containment: Christ's 'two consciousnesses' were consecutive rather than concurrent. While on earth, Christ's consciousness had, for the most part, a human character. His sensations, perceptions, and propositional attitudes, were, in many ways, much like our own. Perhaps he had occasional access to the divine contents of consciousness. This would *not* involve one mind accessing a different mind, far less one consciousness accessing a different consciousness, it would merely involve having the sorts of conscious experiences

mer has to be excluded for reasons that are fairly obvious, but the latter possibility, that one and the same thought occupies both minds at the same time, presents challenges of its own. If, for example, the thought of both minds is in every way the same, it becomes somewhat difficult to say that one mind truly differs from the other. The importance of finding some difference between the two thoughts is further underscored by the intrinsic difference between the thought of an infinite, fully actual, and creative mind, on the one hand, and a finite, potential, and fundamentally passive mind on the other (which we will also have to consider later in specific connection with salvation). Between the extremes of Jesus' thinking identical thoughts in two minds, on the one hand, and his thinking unconnected and disjointed thoughts in these, on the other, is the possibility that he thinks one and the same thought in two distinct ways.[32] This does not mean, of course, that Christ divinely has one thought about one thing at one time, then another. It goes without saying, even in the present context, that God does not have a successive and serial understanding. Nevertheless, we can still suppose that Christ in his human mind thinks thoughts that reflect divine understanding. He conceives of an apposite and limited reflection of the same (infinite) content in a properly human mode. This signifies, then, a human distillation of ineffability, of the divine Es-

---

and states that are typical of God. Perhaps Christ remained omniscient (and omnipotent) while incarnate, but if so, most of his knowledge was not consciously accessible to him. It was, if you like, dormant. It may have guided his actions in certain ways, but only to a limited degree."

32. Cf. Garrigou-Lagrange, "L'unique personnalité," 71. In regard to the two intellects of Christ, he says: "Elles restent toujours réellement distinctes et infiniment distantes, mais pourtant se compénétrent, un peu comme l'air et la lumière."

sence itself as the supreme object of thought and of the truth of things that stand in God as their foundation. With respect to the latter, we cannot risk minimizing the reality that things have in the created order in comparison with their existence in the divine mind, as Meister Eckhart seems to have done. It is true nonetheless, however, that God possesses the truth of created things in a way that is humanly unspeakable. In advance of exploring the soteriological consequences of his double knowing in chapter 2, we should note at this point the fact that Jesus Christ mediates between the ultimate understanding of things in God, on the one hand, and their human expression, on the other, by the coincidence of both in his single Person.[33]

## ATHENS AND JERUSALEM

In this light, we must question approaches that present Christ's human knowing as out of step with the divine intellect. If Jesus has a different understanding of the plan of salvation than the Father has (to which he must accommodate himself in the Garden of Gethsemane, etc.) or if Christ is ignorant of what the Father knows regarding Christ's mission, then the following questions must be answered: Who (or what) has a different understanding from the Father? If an answer to this question is framed in terms of the divine Word, the result is tritheism. If tritheism is avoided, that is, it is recognized that the Word knows what the Father knows, and

33. Several authors have taken up the issue of the mental and linguistic expression of Christ's knowledge. See Maritain, *Grace and Humanity,* 94–95, 103; Maloney, *Knowledge of Christ,* 62, 98–99; Durand, "Science du Christ," 499–500; Glorieux, "Révélation," 35; and Amato, *Gesù il signore,* 396.

the answer is given as the human mind of Christ, two related problems ensue. In the first place, one would have to account for how a faculty (or combination of faculties) of nature can be said to speak—since operations belong to persons and not to natures or faculties—and why the human mind of Christ would be authorized to express itself on behalf of the Person of the Word. In the second place, one would have to explain "where" the Person of the Word is while such action is taking place. It is on a strange condition indeed that we can say that Jesus, even if speaking according to his human lights, did not know the answer to a human question: Jesus' own (omniscient) Person must not have been "there" to provide to his human intellect the requested information.[34] In a case where

34. In substance these observations run along the lines of the well-known condemnation of the Agnoetes, who attributed ignorance to the human Christ, as fundamentally Nestorian by Pope Gregory the Great: DS 476. We must highlight the fact that this line of thought only applies to human questions and humanly expressible answers; it is not at all germane to that which God knows but which would escape the ken of human rationality. Put differently, this consideration does not make Christ's human intellect infinite (and, so, not human). There certainly are things that Jesus cannot humanly know, that is, there are things that he can only know divinely, but these things could never in principle be required of Jesus in a human question or quandary. Ignorance of exclusively divine truths—or truth in an exclusively divine profundity—does not represent a falling into Nestorianism because these simply cannot be communicated as such to Christ in his humanity, no matter how "close" one conceives the hypostatic union to be. The question of Christ's relative human ignorance of God's infinity—that he attains but does not comprehend the divine Essence in his human intellect—is addressed by St. Thomas, whose lead is followed here, in *ST* 3, 10, 1–2. Thomas famously, and I think correctly, says that Jesus does not humanly know of things that God could have created but did not create. It may be objected that a creature, or possible creature, would be a proper object of human knowledge (of which Christ is ignorant), but this is wide of the mark because of the fact that divine creative possibilities, of whatever order, are as such "untranslated" into human thought. In other words, the objection treats divine creational possibilities as if they were already realized forms capable of informing created intellects. For a particularly helpful, synthetic

Jesus is thought to be ignorant, is there no one present who knows the answer to the question?[35]

We can elucidate this issue by returning to the liability just mentioned in supposing that a nature or faculty acts instead of a person. We must always ask *who* is speaking in a Gospel passage in which Christ is taken to profess ignorance. There is ultimately one referent indicated by "Jesus," "the Lord," and the

---

contrast between Thomas and Bonaventure on Christ's human knowledge and nescience, see Eugenio M. Bosco, O.Carm., *La scienza umana del Cristo in San Tommaso e San Bonaventura: Divergenze e concordanze* (Naples: "Tipomeccanica" Marra, 1954), 55–56. For further contrast between the same thinkers, see also Raymond Maloney, S.J., *Knowledge of Christ,* 55–63. Scotus is added to the picture on 64–65. See also Raymond Maloney, S.J., "Mind of Christ," 294, esp. note 24.

35. For an alternative perspective on this question, see Adam, *Christ of Faith,* 275–76, where the Word Incarnate has knowledge potentially but refused to call up this knowledge because it was not to be revealed then. Another contrast is in Jacques Guillet, S.J., *The Consciousness of Jesus,* trans. Edmond Bonin (New York, Paramus, N.J., and Toronto: Newman Press, 1972), 146: "Nothing in the gospels warrants our imagining, behind this human face just like ours, another consciousness for which everything would already be over and done with. To invent, miraculously lodged in the infant of Bethlehem or the workman of Nazareth, a God with infallible perception who could already see the dawn of Easter, would be to introduce into Jesus two persons, two Christs, and dissolve him in myth. If, in Jesus, God is not the one who says 'I,' the one who stands amazed, who worries and is seized by fear, then Jesus is not God but only an impersonator. The Jesus of the gospels exists in real time—ours—and can leave it only by resurrecting." In connection with Mk 13:32 and ignorance of the day or hour, Thomas G. Weinandy, O.F.M., Cap., in "The Human 'I' of Jesus," *Irish Theological Quarterly* 62, no. 4 (1996): 259–68, 265, states: "If the Son as God (under the conditions of a divine 'I') is saying he does not know when the last hour will be, he would be a liar, since, as God the Son, he must know what God the Father knows. However, what is extremely important here is that it actually is the divine Son saying that he does not know when the end will come, and he is speaking the truth precisely because the divine Son, as man, knows, speaks and acts only within the parameters of his human 'I.' The Son can truly say: '*I, who am the Son,* do not know' only because that 'I' is human and not divine." See, finally, Romanus Cessario, O.P., "Incarnate Wisdom and the Immediacy of Christ's Salvific Knowledge," in *Atti del IX Congresso tomistico internazionale, 5: Problemi teologici alla luce dell'Aquinate,* ed. Antonio Piolanti (Vatican City: Libreria Editrice Vaticana, 1991), 338–39.

like, even allowing for a distinction in the aspect under which reference is made. There is only one personal subject, one *he,* who says, undergoes, and does everything attributed to him in the Bible. One hardly needs to labor the point that there is not a distinct human actor alongside or independent of a divine subject, but it is puzzling how often this basic Christian understanding goes unobserved in interpreting the New Testament texts that give us an insight into the character and personality of Christ. Since the preexistent Subject is not replaced by or paired with a new human subject, then to ascribe ignorance to Jesus is to ascribe ignorance to God. If one insists that Jesus did not know the answer to questions leveled at him or that he was ignorant of the facts and exigencies of human reality around him, we must consider that there is hardly anyone else (any other person, any other subject) to whom one ascribes ignorance. In other words, no one in the Gospels ever asks Jesus' human nature a question and Jesus' human nature never speaks. The seemingly innocuous and exegetically "straightforward" attribution of ignorance to the Gospels' Jesus runs up against questions that are very difficult to answer. In this regard, the biblical interpreter who sees Jesus as fundamentally a human person is much more consistent than one who says that Jesus is God but that humanity is speaking in the Gospels.

The present willingness to allow specifically theological considerations to influence our reading of the Gospel Christ seems to be open to the charge of conflating two very different modes of thought and asking one to answer the rather incommensurable questions of the other. Metaphysics and narrative, ontology and Gospel, Athens and Jerusalem: the impermeable demarcation is transgressed in an indelicate and insensitive way. In response to this difficulty, we may offer a few observations. First, the one who claims that Jesus is ignorant on the basis of Scripture usually hopes that his claim is taken by others to be true, that it has traction in the real order of things and not simply as story. *Volens nolens* he or she has already unlocked the ontological with the passkey of "is" and "is not." The second consideration goes along with the first: Are we not justified in asking about the psychology, subjectivity, and metaphysical structure of Christ if he was a real figure whose history affects us today? Does not an intransigent recourse to "genre," "mode of discourse," and so on represent an abnegation of the task of theology? To find Mark and John in a "dialectical tension" or "paradox" is simply to throw up one's hands in response to a serious theological question under the pretense of sophistication. No less precarious is the harmony achieved by demythologizing John or dismissing his Gospel by dating, in discomfiture with his unabashedly high Christology. Finally, it cannot be denied that a person who would like to read the Bible in the mode of pure existentialism brings a priori philosophical commitments to that undertaking no less than does the metaphysical realist.

It is certainly not the case that every theologian or biblical exegete must ask questions of this kind or these questions in particular, but the claim that no one can or should ask such questions in principle seems to stem from an exaggeration of disparity between disciplines. Does Scripture make positive statements? For Catholics, the answer cannot but be in the affirmative and recognition of this in the case of Christ's knowledge does something toward overcoming what is by now a tragic-comic divide in theological disciplines.

## SCRIPTURE

To do justice to the hermeneutic questions involved in the complex of issues with which we are occupied here would no doubt require a separate book. In the context of the theme and parameters of the present study, the goal is much more modest. I have a twofold aim. In terms of method, I will propose one criterion for the interpretation of scriptural texts that seem to bear on the question of Christ's knowledge. In terms of content, I will suggest that this criterion may be applied without violence to the canons of good interpretation. I will endeavor to unfold the matter of method progressively, apace with a discussion of key New Testament passages.

The methodological point that I wish to make is by no means original; in essence it is that Scripture has a meaning-giving context without which it is not finally intelligible. Raymond Brown offers the measured observation that "in Roman Catholic thought there is no need to torture biblical texts in order to find in NT [New Testament] times an awareness of church doctrines articulated in later centuries, even though those doctrines cannot be seen to contradict the NT."[36] Without denying that Catholic understanding of Revelation which seals it within the apostolic period—however we may understand the ever-deeper appropriation and understanding

36. Raymond E. Brown, S.S., *An Introduction to New Testament Christology* (New York and Mahwah, N.J.: Paulist Press, 1994), 30.

of Revelation in subsequent centuries—we cannot but agree with the sentiment behind this admonition. It would be hazardous to claim that the New Testament in no sense knows the truths later articulated by the Magisterium, but it would be naïve to think that the New Testament explicitly knows them *as* the Magisterium articulates them. Brown is among those theologians who do not believe that Magisterial teachings on the Christ's possession of the beatific vision and Jesus' "unlimited"[37] knowledge are "binding dogmatically"[38]—for him we are dealing only with competing theologies in the question of Christ's human knowing. Nevertheless, his basic point about doctrinal statements—and, by extension, theological statements—applies here: we may not expect to find clearly articulated formulae in Scripture that respond to the set of questions raised here *as* they are raised here. For all of the weight this observation carries, it must also be borne in mind that no theological statement can be at once true and openly contradicted by the Bible. The salient question is whether or not the Gospels really teach that Jesus was ignorant, nescient regarding concrete matters, or in error. I will confine my reflections on this question to the raising of several points immediately germane to the question of Christ's human knowing in lieu

37. Brown, *NT Christology,* 29. Elsewhere (41), Brown uses the term "omniscient" to describe a traditional view of Jesus' human intellect. Although examples can be found of this view in the theological tradition (e.g., apparently Fulgentius of Ruspe), generally speaking it is a straw man who claims that Jesus' human knowledge is truly and literally unlimited. Bonaventure came far closer to this view than does any Thomist, but for him Jesus' knowledge was not actual. On this point, in addition to the text from Bosco, *La scienza umana,* already cited, see Riedlinger, *Geschichlichkeit*, 87–89. Cf. *ST* 1, 12, 7 and 3, 10, 1–2.

38. Brown, *NT Christology,* 29, including note 31. Cf. 57–58, note 73, 72.

of elaborating a detailed, positive exegesis of "problematic" passages. These reflections will largely center around the complexity present in those interpretations that favor ignorance or error on Christ's part and the possibility of alternate interpretations.[39] I will deal here by way of adumbration and with representative passages—one in which Jesus seems to learn something and another pair of pericopes in which he is apparently mistaken—in order to suggest that where divergent interpretations are exegetically defensible, other considerations can and should urge one interpretation over others.

Some Gospel passages show Jesus as apparently surprised; surprise is ordinarily predicated on ignorance in some form. The beginning of Mt 14 describes the beheading of John the Baptist by Herod. The pericope ends (v. 12) with the notice that the disciples went to bring word of the execution to Jesus. The succeeding pericope, in which Jesus multiplies food for his listeners, opens (v. 13) with the notice that Jesus, hearing this, went from there by boat to a desolate place by himself.

These verses seem to suggest ignorance on Jesus' part in two ways. In a first way, the disciples bring a report (ἀπήγγειλαν) to Jesus and there is no positive indication in the text, either from the narrator or from the speakers, that Jesus already knows the

39. The interpretive strategy that I hope to underline here is no different from that which Catholics typically employ in, e.g., identifying the meaning of ἀδελφοί ("brothers") in connection with Jesus, as in Mt 12:47, 13:55; Mk 3:31; Lk 8:19–20; and Jn 2:12. From the perspective of exegesis alone, more than one interpretation is possible, but in the light of Tradition and authority Catholics to rule out the word's otherwise legitimate sense as full, blood brothers, since this would preclude Mary's perpetual virginity. While the present case, that of Christ's knowledge and the beatific vision, cannot be said to involve Magisterial authority at the same level, I find the assessment that the Church's teaching on these subjects has no (or no practical) authority for Catholic theologians to be tendentious and misleading.

content of their message. In a second way, the impression of ignorance is reinforced by Jesus' reaction. The message certainly seems to bring Jesus a sorrow that he did not have before hearing the disciples; one naturally concludes that Jesus seeks solace in the desolate place. This is a particularly problematic passage because it cannot be explained as maieutic ignorance (e.g., Jn 4:16–17, Mk 9:33) or in the key of "economic" ignorance (as, somewhat traditionally, in reference to Mt 24:36, Mk 13:32).[40] Jesus seems to be stricken at heart by new information.

This interpretation seems quite plausible, but does it trust too much to our narrative assumptions? Is this the only way to read the passage? Could we not also read this pericope, for example, as presupposing Jesus' real insertion in history and its events and his profound connection to other people? How often are we previously aware of something but find ourselves cut to the quick when it is mentioned aloud? How often, more to point, do others bring to the surface our grief when they come to commiserate with us?

Regarding the fact that Jesus does not stop his disciples from telling him that John the Baptist was dead, there is no particular difficulty. We could point out that the disciples'

40. Cf. Duquoc, *Christologie,* 148, which claims that the interpretation of Christ's "ignorance" as pedagogy goes back to Origen. Francis X. Gumerlock, in "Mark 13:32 and Christ's Supposed Ignorance: Four Patristic Solutions," *Trinity Journal* 28, no. 2 (2007): 205–13, is a fine overview of the controversy surrounding and explanations of Mk 13:32 (and par. Mt 24:36): "No one knows about that day or that hour, neither the angels of the heavens nor the Son but the Father." See also Kevin Madigan, "*Christus Nesciens*? Was Christ Ignorant of the Day of Judgment? Arian and Orthodox Interpretations of Mark 13:32 in the Ancient Latin West," *Harvard Theological Review* 96, no. 3 (2003): 255–78, esp. 259–74. Cf. Anton Vögtle, "Exegetische Erwägungen über das Wissen und Selbstbewusstsein Jesu," in *Gott in Welt: Festgabe für Karl Rahner,* vol. 1, ed. Herbert Vorgrimler (Freiburg im Breisgau, Basel, and Vienna: Verlag Herder KG, 1964), esp. 609–10.

announcement would not have been omitted from the scene because it certainly serves to clue in the reader, move narrative action forward, and transition between pericopes. Beyond this, however, basic human experience suggests that we more often listen to that which we know than to that which we do not know. In sum, neither Jesus' emotional response nor the disciples' belief that they were informing Jesus decisively militates against reading this pericope with Jesus already aware of the Baptist's execution.

None of the foregoing should be taken to gainsay the fact that, *all else being equal,* the interpretation of this pericope that first and most plainly suggests itself is that Jesus did not know that the Baptist had been executed. But it is precisely this *all else being equal* that is lacking in the present case. With few exceptions among exegetes, Scripture studies today require that a text be read without *hermeneutic* (not redactional, etc.) reference to other books in the Bible, except where it draws the latter by paraphrasing, quoting, reusing images, and so on; thus one does not explain Matthew by referring to John. However, since scriptural study generally should enter into the ambit of the theological and the ecclesial, the value of this interpretative norm is marginal and cannot be exercised with rigor. In concrete terms, we can at least say that one book of the Bible cannot be taken to contradict another book in terms of the truth that it really conveys. (That the women in Christ's company arrive at the empty tomb at different times, that there are divergent accounts of Judas's death, etc., are facts very much beside the point that I wish to make here.)

The case here is not for Gospel harmonies that reduce Gospel theologies to exercises in factual accounting, which are more at home in courts of law and newsrooms. But if John provides a true portrait of Jesus[41]—and John's voice is not muffled by a fabric of aprioristic arguments about what in his Gospel can and cannot be taken seriously, then statements such as John 2:25, where Jesus is said to know what is in man without being told, are not irrelevant to how we understand Matthew.[42] The reason for this is simple: Jesus was a concrete, historical figure. Multiple, competing accounts are only possible in the case of fictional characters.

Although much of the research into the historical Jesus has steered clear of theological categories, such quests are not without consequence for theology. Of singular moment for the theological conclusions that I am advancing here are passages that can be taken to imply that Christ was not simply ignorant but mistaken. A particularly difficult passage is Mk 2:26. Here Jesus is responding to Pharisees who have criticized his disciples for reaping on the Sabbath. Jesus answers by referring to the fact that David and his men ate the showbread, or bread of permanent offering, during the time that Abiathar was high priest (the Greek is ἐπὶ Ἀβιαθὰρ ἀρχιερέως). In point of fact, Ahimelech was high priest rather than Abiathar.[43] Of course, if Jesus made a true, factual claim that turned out to be false, it would be difficult to maintain that he possessed the rather complete understanding that I am arguing for here. Let me preface a discussion of this passage by recalling the goals and

41. Cf. Jn 19:35 and 21:24.

42. For a general discussion of the Johannine texts that bear on Christ's knowledge, see Tekippe, "Systematic Understanding," 81–84.

43. 1 Sm 21:2–7.

limits of our investigation. In asking the present question, of whether or not Jesus did make a false, factual claim, the only ambition that I have is to suggest that it is exegetically *permissible*—not exegetically *required*—to think that he did not. Theological considerations and commitments to Church teaching can, again, inform a responsible decision for one or another interpretation among real exegetical possibilities.

For Jesus to have made a false claim in a factual matter, all of the following conditions must hold true: (1) Mark really wrote "when Abiathar was high priest," that is, this phrase is not a scribal interpolation. (Not all of the manuscripts of Mark include these words, although they are probably original.)[44] (2) We should not read "ἱερέως" instead of "ἀρχιερέως" (as in some manuscripts), which would not be inaccurate; Abiathar was priest—not yet high priest—at the time of this incident.[45] (3) Mark's syntax is unambiguous here; his meaning is not *during the time of Abiathar, who was [sometime] high priest,* along the lines suggested by Chrysostom and several copyists, who recast the phrase as "ἐπὶ Ἀβιαθὰρ τοῦ ἀρχιερέως."[46] (4) Jesus does not recall Abiathar instead of Ahimelech because Abiathar was a much more notable personage than Ahimelech during this general period; Jesus' intent was to call to mind the showbread episode without any such adornment.[47] (5) Mark

44. Two good overviews of this problem, which provide details very useful here, are Brown, *NT Christology,* 37–38, and Craig A. Evans, "Patristic Interpretation of Mark 2:26: 'When Abiathar was High Priest,'" *Vigiliae Christianae* 40 (1986): 183–86.

45. See Evans, "Patristic Interpretation," 184.

46. See Evans, "Patristic Interpretation," 183–84.

47. See William G. Most, *The Consciousness of Christ* (Front Royal, Va.: Christendom Publications, 1980), 44–45.

records something at least very close to the *ipsissima verba* of Jesus in this case. If it is true that Jesus' own words are carefully reproduced here—if Jesus' publicly proclaimed something that is manifestly inaccurate—it is curious that apparently no one corrected him on the spot. In this connection, we should be able to provide some explanation for the fact that the Pharisees, evidently well schooled in Scripture, do not seem to notice. Options here are few: we do not see Jesus' interlocutors correct Jesus' error because they demurred from reproaching Jesus, because Mark wants to show the strength of Jesus' response and so omits this compromising detail, or because they shared his mistake. (It would be remarkable if the Pharisees shared an error that was easily detected by Mark's dependents: the copyists, as mentioned, of some manuscripts in which the phrase in question is absent as well as, presumably, Matthew and Luke, in whose accounts this specification does not appear.) In sum, a number of assumptions seem to underlie the notion that Jesus publicly voiced his own ignorance of a well-known story. The matter is not as simple as reading Mk 2:26 alongside 1 Sm 21:2–7. When placed against its alternatives, the interpretation that imputes a factual error to Christ in a historical conversation can hardly claim to be the only solid exegesis of the passage before us.

It is notoriously difficult to discern, in this case and others like it, where Jesus is speaking literally and intends to make a factual claim, on the one hand, from cases in which Jesus speaks in figures and according to common acceptation, on the other. It is striking in this light that even estimable scholars can take exception to the fact that he does not seem to agree, in some cases, with the findings of modern biblical research. Jesus, for example, refers to Jonah as a prophet in Mt 12:39–41, 16:4 and Lk 11:29–32. Brown passes over this objection, very fairly it seems, as not having much weight since Jesus' mention of Jonah cannot be taken as a wholesale endorsement of the historicity of this story.[48] In fact, Brown seems to be onto something important in this stance, even if he does not draw out his explanation. It would be difficult to deny that Jesus accommodated his message to the conceptual and linguistic patterns of his audience. From its early employment in Antiochene theology to the 1964 Pontifical Biblical Commission's statement on the process by which Jesus' revelation is committed to the sacred page (*Sancta Mater Dei*),[49] theology has benefited immeasurably from the notion of divine condescension or accommodation. We can go a step further, however. Without prejudice to the fullness of his knowledge, Jesus so fully entered the human condition—not merely the state of humanity in the abstract but the concrete circumstances of a time, place, family, and people—that he was wont to direct the flow and expression of his astonishing understanding along the courses and channels typical of his contemporaries. These modes of thought and styles of expression were habituated in him in the course of experience.[50] This point is not to be understood on the model of a member of European nobility

48. Brown, *NT Christology,* 39.

49. Cf. *Dei verbum,* 19.

50. Cf. Kaiser, *Das Wissen Jesu Christi,* 289: "Der Grund für die Verflochtenheit des Geisteslebens Jesu mit der Geisteswelt der damaligen Zeit und Umwelt liegt in der Struktur menschlicher Geistigkeit überhaupt: sie ist wesentlich *dialogisch* geprägt." See also 290.

who imitates the accent and idioms of the members of lower social classes in speaking with them. In living as a first-century Galilean Jew, Jesus picks up the conventions of Galilean Jews without—it hardly needs to be said—being strictly confined to them. Although much too much is made of Lk 2:52 in regard to the question of Jesus' understanding,[51] the fact that Jesus encounters and appropriates ways to express that which he understands can contribute to an explanation of this verse. Returning to the question of Jonah, then, it is not surprising if Jesus makes use of a working understanding of Jonah in the fashion of Haggadah, in which rigid distinctions between the pious embellishment of a story and its historical kernel would be out of place and anachronistic.

Let us return a final time to the methodological point. It is well known that, perhaps inspired by an equivalent movement in the physical sciences, in recent decades philosophy, theology, and biblical studies have alike abandoned the fiction of a neutral-observer standpoint. It seems quite evident that any attempt to answer the question of Christ's human knowing from Scripture alone invariably involves, with a greater or lesser degree of transparency, the finding of a canon within the canon. If taken as individual data, scriptural references (or possible references) to that which Jesus knew or did not know can be assembled in widely divergent configurations to suit the tastes of the exegete. Without pushing this comparison too far, we may liken treatment of the present issue

51. With no advertence to the place that this stylized phrase holds in the architecture of Luke's step parallelism between John the Baptist and Jesus, the refrain that Jesus "increased in wisdom" is regularly used as a proof-text in favor of ignorance or nescience on the part of Jesus.

to the fourth-century contest with Arianism. The Arians and the Semi-Arians did not lack an apparent biblical foundation to support their position and it was not merely the counter-quoting of Scripture that proved successful in refuting their position. Rather, the broad context in which Scripture finds a place was urgently brought to bear on the reading of Scripture. It is not only that the same strategy is warranted in the present case; more than this, the very enterprise of theology is impossible without it. We cannot object to the fact that theology brings preconvictions to the reading of the Gospels; we can only question the kinds of preconvictions that it brings.

In this section, I have emphasized the narrative unity of Jesus Christ that is conditioned by the fact that he is a historical Person. Since there is only one character described in the New Testament and by the Church, everything said about him in these loci must be consistent, else at least some of it is untrue. We will look at the question of Christ's unity again in the next section from a very different perspective; we will move from narrative unity to personal unity and find that these two issues are closely related. Let us conclude the present argument, then, before moving on. One can only insist on a reading of some passages in Mark or Matthew as compromising Christ's knowledge at the expense of consistency with John. The supposition that one must choose between Mark and John—or, extending this to the ecclesial, between Matthew and the Magisterium—fails to take broader considerations into account. The interpretation of many verses in Scripture along the lines that I have suggested is admittedly arduous, but the contention that it is impossible represents an overly hasty dismissal of many other realities that have to be taken into account if the Bible is not to be read as common literature. When one takes Tradition and the Magisterium into consideration and employs an intertextual approach to Scripture, it becomes clear that in the matter of interpreting certain scriptural passages concerning Christ's human knowledge, there is no choice between an easy interpretation and a forced interpretation. The only decision is between the arduous and the incoherent.[52]

52. One is reminded here of the saying of Sir Arthur Conan Doyle's Sherlock Holmes in *A Scandal in Bohemia*: "Once you eliminate the impossible, whatever remains, no matter how improbable, must be the truth." Somehow it must be possible to make sense of everything together. No authoritative claim or text is an embarrassment to theology. We may take it is axiomatic that some understanding of Christ's psychological structure and characteristics is capable of holding all of the texts together. Without claiming that Maloney supports any specific conclusion or observation that I put forward, I basically agree with the following observation: "[T]he New Testament cannot answer our question [of Christ's knowledge and consciousness] on its own. [T]he evidence to be gathered from that source is ambivalent, now favouring one side of the argument, now another. In so far as an eventual answer can be given at all, it can come only by taking the New Testament in combination with the subsequent dogmatic tradition." (I would qualify that New Testament texts do not at bottom favor one then another, but interpretations of these do.) Cf. Albert Schweitzer, *The Quest of the Historical Jesus: A Critical Study of Its Progress from Reimarus to Wrede,* trans. W. Montgomery (New York: Macmillan, 1948), 7: "It may be maintained by the aid of arguments drawn from the sources that the self-consciousness of Jesus underwent a development during the course of His public ministry; it may, with equally good grounds, be denied. For in both cases the arguments are based upon little details in the narrative in regard to which we do not know whether they are purely accidental, or whether they belong to the essence of the facts. In each case, moreover, the experimental working out of the hypothesis leads to a conclusion which compels the rejection of some of the actual data of the sources. Each view equally involves a violent treatment of the text." Schweitzer's statement is insightful and succinct, yet (without accusing Schweitzer on this point) we should be on guard against relegating parts of Scripture to the "accidental" and against dismissing some of its statements in order to affirm others; the point is to untangle the knot, not to cut it. *Enchiridion symbolorum: Definitionum et declarationum de rebus fidei et morum,* 36th (Barcelona, Freiburg

## ANTIOCH AND ALEXANDRIA

It is not intuitively clear that a cogent account of Christ's personal unity depends on attributing to him a full human understanding. Few people would suppose that either we can explain Christ as one Person or we can describe him as nescient, but that we encounter obstacles if we try to do both. The questions surrounding Christ's understanding are seldom formed in such stark contrasts. More often we observe a nuanced and subtle account of Christ's nescience that rests on a concept of—for lack of a better term—divine occlusion.[53]

im Breisgau, and Rome: Herder, 1976) and *The Christian Faith in the Doctrinal Documents of the Catholic Church,* 7th ed. (New York: Alba House, 2001) (hereafter ND) list several texts from the Magisterium pertinent to the present discussion. These include interventions from Pope Vigilius (ND 619/4, [231]; DS 419), Gregory the Great (ND 624–26 [237–39]; DS 474–76), Pius X (ND 650/32–35 [255]; DS 3432–35), the Holy Office under Benedict XV (ND 651/1–3 [256–57]; DS 3645–47), and Pius XII (ND 661 [261], DS 3812).

53. Ivor Davidson sees a similar trend in regards to Christ's volition; see Davidson, "Not My Will," 195: "The monothelites against whom Maximus argued could not conceive of how there could be a distinction of wills in Christ without some form of opposition between them. On their reasoning, divine purpose had to overwhelm human willing if the Incarnation was to be confessed as a divine act. More modern forms of monothelitism may tend to take the opposite approach: if human willing is to be conceived of as free, it must exist on its own terms, unconstrained by divine forces." Cf. Thomas G. Weinandy, O.F.M., Cap., "The Human 'I' of Jesus," *Irish Theological Quarterly* 62, no. 4 (1996): 259–68, 266: "What the Incarnation entails, and the tradition and Councils confirm, is that he who embraced a human 'I,' and so willed, thought, spoke and was conscious of himself within the confines of that human 'I,' was the eternal Son. The identity of Jesus is the Son, but the manner or mode of that identity is as man.... [T]he divine Son (the subject/person) ..., as incarnate, lives, experiences himself, and expresses himself in a totally human manner—with a human self-identity, under the conditions of a human 'I.'" Cf. also 263–64: "[T]he divine Son, as incarnate, not only lives and acts within the confines of a human will and human intellect, but he also is conscious and knows himself within the confines of a human self-consciousness." Cf. further 268, footnote 15. Cf., finally, Weinandy, "Jesus' Filial Vision," 194–96.

Although much more sophisticated and refined than ancient Antiochene thought, which tended to make of Christ's humanity a full subject in itself, occlusion theories are subject to some of the same fundamental liabilities. Nothing significant is improved, moreover, by adjusting the degree to which divinity is occluded to Christ's human thought. We will return to a specific type of occlusion theory later on, so let it suffice for the present to indicate a general problem with this idea. This notion—which we may understand as an economic (as opposed to ontological) human monophysitism—betrays a fundamental misunderstanding of person and nature.

We scarcely touched on the relationship between these capital concepts above. It is worthwhile at this point to begin to be more specific. A solid starting point is the classical formulation *Operatio est personae,* acting belongs to persons. This formulation would be incomplete without specifying how it is that persons act: persons act through natures.[54] The person is the principle that acts (*principium quod*) and nature is the principle by which the person acts (*principium quo*). We must be careful in how we understand this; we would render this

54. On the importance of this idea, see, e.g., John McDermott, S.J., "The Christologies of Karl Rahner, II," *Gregorianum* 67, no. 2 (1986): 297–327, 311–15, and 319–26. McDermott's engaging criticism of Rahner highlights the need for a cogent and clear use of "person" and "nature." I am also grateful to Fr. McDermott for attuning me to the significance of this distinction in private correspondence. For a different perspective on Rahner's idea, see David M. Coffey, "The Theandric Nature of Christ," *Theological Studies* 60 (1999): 405–31, 413, including note 23. For a discussion of the relationship between person and nature in Pope Leo the Great's Flavian Tome and its subsequent conciliar and theological reception, see Demetrios Bathrellos, *The Byzantine Christ: Person, Nature, and Will in the Christology of Saint Maximus the Confessor,* Oxford Early Christian Studies (Oxford: Oxford University Press, 2004), 175–89.

idea unintelligible and indefensible if we were to imagine that nature is simply some sort of accessory to personality. Persons do not use natures as instruments in the strict sense. The nature of a person is not an outcropping from or extension of personhood, however closely we try to conceive thus of their association. It is, rather, the intelligible and existential concretion of personhood. There are no persons who are not in and of a (rational) nature. That is, personhood in precision from a specific nature remains nothing more than an unreal abstraction, devoid, really, of any but a least-common-denominator definition.

Nature, accordingly, is not something that may simply be switched on or off by person. Personhood (with due apologies for mixing metaphors) is not a sort of neutral light that can be directed through a colored lens consistently, at intervals, or not at all but that fundamentally remains separate from the lens.[55] A closer approximation is in the way that we speak of light and color together; although color and light are conceptually separable, in the existential order light is simply absent apart from color. Color defines light, but color is not present except in il-

55. Cf. the summary of Galtier's thought on this point in connection with Christ in Cé, "Discussione," 277: "Viene ... esclusa una concezione che attribuisca alla Persona dei mezzi d'azione propri, indipendentemente dalle due nature, che essa potrebbe manovrare, or l'una or l'altra, a suo piacimento, come si evita di ridurre la natura umana a un puro automa privo d'un dinamismo proprio." Cf. also Davidson, "Not My Will," 198: although Davidson emphasizes (in some disharmony with Galtier) that abstract natures do not will (rather, the Word incarnated wills), he otherwise substantially maintains the same relationship of person to nature in action. He says: "It is not that his personhood exists in any sort of detachment from his natures, opting, as it were, to deploy qualities from one or other according to whim (it is wrong to think, for example, of the incarnate Christ as 'using' one will at one moment, the other at the next)."

lumination. In the same way, rational nature is not a feature of personhood; it is rather the defining reality of personhood.

Be this as it may, we must acknowledge here that the case of the Incarnate Word presents a special—even in some sense exceptional—case, and this would still be true even if it were possible to prescind here from the weighty issue of divine immutability. The human nature of the Word is not the essentially defining feature of the Word; if it were, the Word would have existed imperfectly, at least apart from the Incarnation and, with this, the lines would begin to blur between humanity and divinity, creature and Creator. As the Word exists from all eternity apart from the human nature of Christ, so the Word remains free to act specifically, and in some way exclusively, as God even after the historical moment of Incarnation.

Are we then not falling back to the image that we have just ruled out, in which the divine Person stands as a kind of neutral light that may, or may not, shine through the lens of his humanity? Is this problem not given an additional heft with the recognition that the Son may also act—or, more to the point, suffer—in his human nature alone? In short, does it not seem that we can rule out this alternating-lenses approach only for the strictly "theandric" (divine and human) actions of Christ—and for these only tenuously—and not at all for his properly divine or properly human actions?

The comparison with accidents that St. Thomas evokes in discussing a related question in the *Tertia pars* is helpful for focusing our reflections toward an answer here.[56] Just as a human person continues to bear, underlie, or even to be his ac-

56. *ST* 3, 2, 2–3.

cidents, even when he does not employ them, so also Christ does not cease being a man when he, in undivided action with the other Trinitarian Persons, holds the world in being by his creative will. A man who is white remains white while he is a baker, but he is not a baker qua white. By analogy, Christ is God while suffering, but he does not suffer as God.

The comparison of accidents to nature is obviously imperfect, but it is capable of showing us that a person does not cease being what it is when it acts in a way that does not employ one of its accidents or even, by extension, its quiddity (if, and only if, it has more than one of these). The Incarnate Word may refrain from an action proper to one of his natures without disengaging that nature itself. The distinction between nature and the acts that issue through a nature (as *principium quo*) is crucial to answering other questions in the same line.

One final issue must be raised in this immediate vein. With substantial support by the Magisterium, theology traditionally describes actions of divine Persons vis-à-vis the created order as common to all three Persons.[57] The rule that God's causality is undivided makes sense in light of the fact that the Son does not *have* a power distinct from that of the Father or Spirit by which he can act in independence of them; each Trinitarian Person *is* the very same power and this power is coterminous with the divine Essence.[58] Just as the divine Essence cannot

57. See Pope Vigilius, 552 (DS 415), Pope Pelagius I, 557 (DS 441), Pope Martin I, 649 (DS 501), Toledo XI, 675 (DS 531 and 535), Pope Agatho, 680 (DS 542, 546–47), Lateran IV, 1215 (In *Firmiter*, DS 800), the Council of Florence, 1441 or 1442 (In the Decree for the Jacobites, DS 1330–31).

58. It should be well noted that Trinitarian processions do not fall under the rubric of God's causality or acts toward creation.

be divided (into three gods), so neither can divine power be proper to one Person to the exclusion of the others. Nor can one Person "tap into" the divine power alone, because this would suggest that the divine Essence is a thing apart from and more primordial than the three Persons. Although this is not an undemanding consideration, it enjoys a certain simplicity in that each Person is the full possession of the divine Nature. The problem of person and nature is more difficult when we combine this idea with the need to maintain the personal singularity of the Word's human actions. A succinct and paradoxical way of exemplifying this problem is to recall that theology has generally considered the giver of the beatific vision to be the undivided Trinity and the recipient of the same to be uniquely the Person of the Word. Since seeing the beatific vision is an act outside of the processions of the immanent Trinity, how can it not be common to the whole Trinity? To clarify this issue, we must bear in mind that—just as rational natures concretize persons—so also do natures specify the actions that belong to persons. Act are from persons, but they are specified by form and nature.[59] Thus, the human action of Christ (as well as the human aspect of a theandric action) is, qua act, of the human-natural order. The one seeing (or eating, or dying) is the Person of the Word according to his human nature.[60] Human nature specifies the work performed such

59. *ST* 3, 19, 1, ad 3m.

60. In *ST* 3, 19, 1, ad 1m Aquinas quotes Pseudo-Dionysius approvingly to the effect that the whole Trinity works the divine operations of Christ, while the Father and the Spirit do not so share in his human operations; these belong to the Second Person alone. Héris outlines Jean Galot's sympathetic attempt to understand this idea and brings it to the following question: How can a divine I operate

that, while it is the work of the divine Son, it is not a properly divine work. If divine power is in no way invoked, no reason suggests that the Persons would act together. The only Person who can act apart from divine power is the one who has also a nondivine nature. Thus, the attribution of human actions to the Word alone does not violate the rule that the works of the Trinity in creation are not proper to individual Persons: *Opera Trinitatis ad extra indivisa sunt.*[61]

## CONSCIOUSNESS, CONSCIOUSNESSES, AND UNDIVIDED WORK OF THE TRINITY

Very roughly, from the fourth to the nineteenth centuries the *Opera Trinitatis* principle held a central and relatively unchallenged place in theology. Similarly, theologians have been generally comfortable in saying that Christ's human actions do not directly involve the Father and the Holy Spirit. However, the model that I have just outlined is not the only way

in and through a purely human intelligence and will? If divine causality itself is invoked here, we are dealing with the common causality of the Trinity instead of with human action proper to the Son. Héris employs this problem to emphasize, along Galtier's lines, nature as responsible for action. See Héris, "Sur la psychologie," 466–68.

61. St. Augustine's *Sermon 52* vividly shows that the great champion of this maxim was not insensitive to the uniqueness of Christ's human actions in its regard. There is a provocative range of thought in the twentieth century on this issue and how it applies to Christology. Lonergan holds, with substantial support culled from Denzinger, that whatever a divine Person produces through efficient causality is common. As for his operations as subsisting in a human nature, the Word (alone) acts: see Lonergan, *Constitution of Christ*, 230–31. Cf. Maritain, *Grace and Humanity*, 52–53. Parente adheres to the unity of divine action *ad extra* only in the case of efficient causality; in the case of formal causality, it is "terminativamente propria": see Cé, "Discussione," 292. However, Diepen, *L'Emmanuel*, 179–81, claims that Parente's thought implies an efficient causality proper to the Word, even in the case of truly theandric actions.

of combining these two ideas. Paul Galtier, Charles-Vincent Héris, and Luigi Jammarrone are notable proponents of the view that the *Opera Trinitatis* rule should be matched to the notion of a proper actor in Christ other than the Word in order to preserve the truth that human actions are not common to the Trinity. For them, because God cannot act otherwise than as one *ad extra* (vis-à-vis creation), the only way to say that human actions belong to Christ alone is to argue that the divine Word does not truly perform them. This view is joined to a third claim, which is less commonly accepted than the *Opera Trinitatis* axiom and the proper character of Christ's human actions: the Father, Son, and Holy Spirit do not have distinct consciousnesses. This notion furthers the assertion that the Word is not the center of human action in Christ by suggesting that neither is the Word the "psychological" center in Christ. The human consciousness of Christ, rather than divine consciousness, is personally unifying and individuating.[62]

62. See Jammarrone, *L'Unità psicologica,* 156: the Trinity has one consciousness; the Word knows that he is incarnate by the same consciousness by which the Father and Spirit know the same. Thus the divine consciousness cannot be the psychological center in Christ. On 195 he says, perhaps in some tension with the aforementioned statement, that each Person "*possiede ... la coscienza divina secondo la proprietà personale*" (italics his). Cf. 300–301 where, summarizing his earlier conclusions, he says that there is an improper sense in which we can say that Son has personal consciousness, but that Jesus' psychological center is really in the human nature. The perception that he is God and man is most properly rooted in his human intellect. See also the summary material on 302: Jesus' identity is known by perceptions that are referred to the I of the Word, but the beatific vision's strengthening of the human intellect allows this identity to be perceived directly. Thus, while the unity of consciousness comes about by both consciousnesses, this integration is due more properly to the human consciousness. Also valuable in this general connection are 197, 205–6, et passim. Cé, "Discussione," 275–76, reports Galtier's view that the psychological center of Christ is his human (not divine) consciousness. The consciousness that laces together psychologically that which is

Although Galtier is certainly on a solid foundation in urging the indispensability of the *Opera Trinitatis* rule, we have just seen that this rule can be respected without denying that it is the Word who humanly acts. The premise accepted by Galtier and others regarding the unity of divine consciousness, however, is not easily dismissed. How do we maintain, with the Council of Florence,[63] etc., that in the Trinity all is one except where relations of opposition intervene while attributing distinct consciousnesses to the Trinitarian Persons? If the Father has a self-awareness that the Son does not have ("I am the Father"), then can we still maintain that the Father and the Son are identical with respect to everything except their opposed relation? The condition of this would be making notional consciousness identical in every way to relation. Yet—even allowing for the analogical character of theology—is this not stretching our words beyond their real sense? On the other hand, if the Father cannot be aware as Father of his distinction from the Son, then are not his distinction and identity compromised? Short of rejecting any application (even analogical) of the idea of consciousness to God, these are not easy questions to answer. Yet it does not seem that we must answer them here in order to see that Galtier missteps in

distinct ontologically is not the divine consciousness. See also 276, note 16, for a list of theologians in favor of and opposed to the idea of distinct consciousnesses for the Trinitarian Persons. Cé reports further on 291 that Parente, unlike Galtier, thinks that there are relative Trinitarian consciousnesses. Herman Diepen, in *L'Emmanuel*, 182, confirms that for Parente there are distinct consciousnesses ("au sens relatif"), while "au sens absolu" there is a unique consciousness. Cf. Jammarrone, *L'Unità psicologica*, 42 for Parente's view, and 62 for Lonergan's acceptance of distinct consciousnesses. Lastly, Natalino Spaccapelo, in "Coscienza," 29, supports the idea of separate notional consciousnesses.

63. DS 1330.

making Christ's human consciousness his determinatively individuating consciousness. The Word can have no need of an individuating or identifying principle outside of himself and the presence of an assumed nature can change nothing in this regard. Galtier, moreover, gives the impression that at least psychologically it is the human nature that assumes the Word in bringing him into its proper awareness.

We have already seen that the position of Galtier and his followers maintains (1) the unity of divine causality, (2) actions proper to the humanity of Christ, (3) and a single divine consciousness that makes recourse to Christ's human intellect indispensable in regard to psychological unity. The fourth leg underpinning this structure is a polemic against the divine hegemony of the Word. The Word's rule over the human will of Christ would compromise *Opera Trinitatis.*[64] Instead, we should see Christ's will as autonomous. Human liberty—and, so, authenticity—would be threatened by specific influence of the Word on the human will of Christ.[65]

Some theologians, however, do in fact conceive of divine hegemony as hegemony of the Word in particular. Jean Galot and Pietro Parente represent this conception.[66] They mean to

64. For the connection between *Opera Trinitatis* and the hegemony of the Word, see Galtier, "Conscience humaine," 238: "'Régler,' contrôler, diriger, donner une impulsion, c'est bien encore agir *ad extra*."

65. Héris is representative of Galtier's followers in arguing that Christ cannot have a human free will if the Word governs his actions in any way; see Héris, "Problème de christologie," 674. See also Charles-Vincent Héris, "A propos de la psychologie humaine du Christ," *Revue Thomiste* 51 (1951): 465–68, and Jammarrone, *L'Unità psicologica,* 298 and 300. See, finally, Cé, "Discussione," 277, which reproduces Galtier's criticism of a unique influence of the Word.

66. See Diepen, *L'Emmanuel,* 20–21, 180, and 261. See also Cé, "Discussione," 290–91. Demetrios Bathrellos, in *Byzantine Christ,* 164, suggests that Parente—in

apply the personal influence of the Word only to Christ's human actions; divine actions remain undivided.[67] Galot also argues that there is no question of the whole Trinity moving the human will or psychology of Christ.[68] While we cannot agree with Galot on every feature of his idea here, the validity of one of its implications should be clear in light of our discussion of action above: this Person, the Word, moves himself humanly.

Diepen, on the other hand, places great emphasis on the whole Trinity's exercise of hegemony with respect to Christ's human nature.[69] There are dangers and advantages to this po-

---

Uso e significato del termine θεοκίνητος nella controversia monothelistica," *Revue des études byzantines* 11 (1953)—interprets St. Maximus along these lines. On the question of whether Maximus really thinks of hegemony in terms of the common operation of the Trinity or as proper to the Word, see 166, which produces texts that show significant ambiguity here. On 168–69, 172, Bathrellos attempts to resolve this ambiguity.

67. Cf. Latour, "Imago Dei invisibilis," 251–52, which puts forward the argument, not exclusive to Latour, that the Word can exercise a distinct influence on the created nature on the precision that this would not be efficient causality but rather exemplary and formal causality. One wonders whether there is not a profound equivocation between the way that Latour uses these terms and their traditional meaning. Furthermore, on what grounds would one argue that "opera" do not include "influences" that go by a name other than "efficient causes"? Cf. Lonergan, *Constitution of Christ,* 230–31, 240–41. Cf. also David M. Coffey, "Quaestio Disputata: Response to Neil Ormerod, and Beyond," *Theological Studies* 68 (2007): 900–915, 909.

68. See Galot, "Psychologie," 355–58. There exists a range of thoughts about and criticisms of Galot's restriction of action in connection with the humanity of Christ to the Word alone. See Héris, "Problème de christologie," 674–75. Cf. Diepen, *L'Emmanuel*, 20–29, esp. 28. Cf. also Haubst, "Welche Ich?" 11–12, 17–18. Although Galtier emphasizes the unity of Trinitarian action in Christ, he does not deny all influence of the Word; see Galtier, "Conscience humaine," 237.

69. Diepen, *L'Emmanuel*, 205, argues that Jesus' human volitional dependence (on divine hegemony) does not imply that the Word alone governs, apart from the other two Persons; in this connection, he quotes Scotus's Oxford Commentary, *Verbum nullam causalitatem habet super actum voluntatis creatae in Christo, quam non habeat tota Trinitas* (Op. ox., III, d. 17, q. 1, n. 4.) On 272–73 he notes that *Haurietis aquas* does not speak in terms of submission of the human will to the

sition. We can have no real hesitancy about common action of the Trinity with respect to Christ as man in terms of grace and as first act, although direct voluntary movement belongs to a person.[70] To balk at unified Trinitarian action of any sort with respect to Christ in his humanity betrays a misunderstanding of secondary causality and mutatis mutandis would render God's influence on the saints unintelligible.

Without claiming that Galot and Diepen see eye to eye, we can say that in some sense both of their positions have something to offer. The metaphysically primordial mover of the human will of Christ is the Person to whom it belongs, although we may add that Christ's human actions are remotely willed and actualized transcendently by the Trinitarian Persons in their common will. It is God the Son alone who humanly fulfills the divine will that originates in the Father and so is common to all of the Trinitarian Persons.[71]

We will return to Galtier's thought in the next section. It

Word but of submission of the human will to the divine Will. Cf. 20–21, where Diepen rejects the view of Capreolus (In III Sent., d. 12., q. 1, a. 3, t. 5)—which Parente, Galot, et al. support in some measure—that the humanity is more the instrument of the Word than of the other Persons. In this conception, the Word would move the humanity as the proximate efficient cause (as the soul moves the hand, in contrast to how one hand moves another), while the Father and Holy Spirit move the humanity as prime and remote mover. See, lastly, Jammarrone, *L'Unità psicologica,* 53, and Galot, "Psychologie," 355–56 (which quotes Herman Diepen, "La psychologie humaine du Christ selon saint Thomas d'Aquin," *Revue Thomiste* 50 [1950]: 515–62, 538): for Diepen, the divine causality that produces human acts in Christ is the Son's only by appropriation—strictly speaking, it is common to the Trinitarian Persons.

70. Galot, "Psychologie," 355, indicates that Diepen does, in fact, believe that human actions are proper to the Word, while the divine actions that elicit these are common.

71. For a seemingly contrasting view, see White, "Voluntary Action," 528–29 et passim.

is worthwhile to summarize what we have gained in looking at his thought before doing so. Galtier's aims of preserving the unity of God's causality—which concern he shares with Diepen—and protecting Christ's human freedom are laudable beyond doubt. However, he does not need to conceive of Christ's human nature as a semiautonomous actor in order to defend these ideas.[72] In addition to the general problems and concerns in Galtier's approach just adumbrated, his description of Jesus as actor encounters difficulties in accounting for the unity of Christ's action. We will begin to see in the next section that these difficulties bear consequences for soteriology.

## NATURE AND ACTION

We have already seen in passing that Galtier's Christology places great emphasis on nature as the principle of perfection.

"It belongs to the person to act through nature" (*ST* 3, 19, 1, ad 3m). Is it not to their natures that persons, whatever these may be, owe whatever traits—intelligence, freedom, self-awareness—that account for their superiority and place them higher than those beings without personality? That which differentiates things from each

72. Jean-Jacques Latour, in "Imago Dei invisibilis," 228–30, suggests that historically theologians have chosen between strict emphasis on the mystery of the Trinity and on that of the hypostatic union. On 228 we read: "Rencontrant ce double mystère, certains sont davantage portés à mettre l'accent sur l'étroitesse de l'unité personnelle, quitte à distendre quelque peu les relations trinitaires et l'unité de l'essence divine; les autres, pour mieux respecter l'unité de la nature incréée, conçoivent de façon plus lâche le rapport entre la nature humaine et la personne du Verbe. Il faut remarquer que, sur ce point, la position adoptée en christologie est logiquement solidaire de la perspective suivant laquelle on envisage la Trinité." My point here is precisely that no such decision is necessary or, more to the point, acceptable.

other consists in the gifts and qualities of their own natures. Therefore, far from it being true that the person determines the mode of acting, the behavior, of its nature, it is exactly the other way around: person depends on nature.[73]

Nature is a concept far more central than is person for Galtier. Héris supports this importance by clarifying nature's primacy in the order of action. Persons do not act, strictly speaking, but—as hypostatic—nature acts. The notion of person is not peripheral to the question of action, according to the position rooted in Galtier's thought, but person is the reality of nature. Person here emerges as the condition, rather than the source, of action.[74]

This position is nearly the inverse of the one supported

73. "'*Operari est personae a natura*' (III, q. 19, a. 1, ad 3m). N'est-ce pas à leur nature que les personnes, quelles qu'elles soient, sont redevables de tout ce qui—intelligence, liberté, conscience—fait leur supériorité et les met au-dessus des êtres sans personnalité? Ce que les différencie entre elles, ce sont les dons et qualités de leurs natures propres. Loin donc qu'une personne détermine le mode d'agir, le comportement, de sa nature, c'est très exactement d'elle que dépend le sien"; see Galtier, "Conscience humaine," 234. Cf. 241: "Sans doute, est-ce toujours la personne qui est autonome et libre. Mais son autonomie, sa liberté, ne tient-elle pas précisément à celle de sa volonté?"

74. See Héris, "Problème de christologie," 674: "La subsistance est condition de l'action, selon le principe: *Actiones sunt suppositorum,* elle n'en est pas la source. Elle donne à l'être concret son unité existentielle, et le place en tel état qu'étant posé dans l'existence il puisse agir. Mais le véritable principe de l'action dans un être, la source première de son activité, c'est sa nature, car elle seule, la nature, possède des puissances et des facultés d'où peuvent jaillir l'action et le mouvement par lesquels un être se porte vers la fin. '*La nature est principe du mouvement*' dira S. Thomas, après Aristote." Cf. 675: "[L]a nature est le principe d'où sort l'action … elle est vraiment ce *par quoi* le suppôt agit." Again on 675, he says: "Quand donc nous disons que la personne ou le suppôt agissent, nous signifions par là que la nature concrète, que la nature hypostasiée agit, mais l'activité jaillit de la nature et non de l'hypostase." Marco Cé, in "Discussione," 302, provides a solid summary of how Galtier et al. understand operation: "[L]a natura è principio dell'azione e del moto, ma non si può attuare se non è sussistente, se non è persona."

above, where we considered nature to be the concrete reality definitive of person. For Galtier's position, person is really the underlying condition for nature. While it cannot be denied that rational natures do not exist apart from personhood and that persons do not exist except in rational natures, the present question is not simply one of where one puts the accent mark. In the position outlined before, a "who" acts and that "who" is of such-and-such whatness. In Galtier's understanding, a "what" acts, on the condition of being a "who." We will continue to draw out soteriological concerns at stake in the unity of Christ's Person as actor in later chapters, but we may draw attention cursorily to the difficulty of considering salvation as having been achieved by two "whats" that happen to belong to the same suppositum.

In light of this concept of acting natures and in accord with the concern to protect Christ's human freedom, Galtier and his followers are naturally apt to isolate a sphere of independent psychological unity in the God-man.[75] We have already

75. See Cé, "Discussione," 276: Since the Person cannot properly be said to act in Galtier's understanding, it is the principle of union in Christ on the ontological level but not on the level of operation. Thus, the two natures remain distinct in their operations and one is not subordinate to the other; each is spontaneous. Cf. Haubst, "Welche Ich?" 11. Cf. also Galtier, "Conscience humaine," 243–44, for Galtier's clarification that he does not see Christ's humanity as a separate subject. To round out this picture, see also 229, which says that Jesus certainly had a human "moi" and a divine "moi"; having more than one "me" is, in fact, not so foreign to ordinary human experience: "[S]'est manifestée en lui la dualité des actes ou des états psychiques, donc des 'moi' psychologiques, qui, chez tous les êtres humains, caractérise les luttes et les victoires de leur être moral." Cf. Galot, "Psychologie," 348: there is one "moi," but consciousness of this "moi" takes a different coloration in the human intellect than it does in the divine. Cf. also Garrigou-Lagrange, "L'unique personnalité," 68–69: there is no "moi humain" or a "personnalité humaine psychologique." Cf. Jammarrone, *L'Unità psicologica,* 285–92 et passim, on the impossibility of an independent, human psychological ego. On the impossibility of Jesus' being two egos, see Amato, *Gesù il signore,* 378–79.

considered the fact that the human consciousness of Christ provides the principle of his identity in this view. This would be largely inconceivable apart from a kind of independence on the level of nature and consciousness.[76]

Yet perhaps we do not have to see the human consciousness of Christ as self-identifying or understand natures to act in order to affirm some kind of psychological duality in the Word Incarnate. Pius XII's 1951 encyclical *Sempiternus Rex Christus,* in the history of its editing, is often indicated as having left the issue of Christ's psychology open to such a possibility. The relevant passage reads:

> Although nothing stands in the way of more profoundly investigating the humanity of Christ, even by psychological and rational methods, nevertheless, in difficult studies of this kind, there are not lacking those who leave behind old ideas more than they ought in order to build up new ones and they misuse the authority and definition of the Council of Chalcedon to sustain their research.
>
> In this way, these persons exalt the state and condition of the human nature of Christ to the point that it seems to be a kind of subject in itself, **, as if in it the Person of the Word himself did not subsist.[77]

76. For Galtier and his followers, psychological independence is not ontological distinction. Héris, in "Problème de christologie," 675, seeks to clarify this point: "[A]utre chose est *une conscience psychologique,* constituée par des phénomènes de vie intérieure dont l'esprit humain fait l'expérience, et autre chose *la personnalité ontologique* qui n'est autre que le Verbe lui-même." See also Cé, "Discussione," 286, 293–94, and 297–98.

77. "Quamvis nihil prohibeat quominus humanitas Christi, etiam psychologica via ac ratione, altius investigetur, tamen in arduis huius generis studiis non desunt qui plus aequo vetera linquant, ut nova astruant et auctoritate ac definitione Chalcedonensis Concilii perperam utantur, ut a se elucubrata suffulciant.

Hi humanae Christi naturae statum et conditionem ita prohevunt ut eadem reputari videatur subiectum quoddam sui iuris, **, quasi in ipsius Verbi persona non subsistat." Diepen, *L'Emmanuel*, 264, reproduces the text as quoted here and

That which seemed to be a rather overt condemnation of Galtier's notion of psychological independence in the first version (which included "saltem psychologicae" ["at least psychologically"]), was not carried over into the document's final edition. The dialing back of this indictment seems to many to represent a willingness to entertain at least some distinctiveness in the human psychology of Christ vis-à-vis the divine intellect of the Logos.

Without construing the human psychology of Christ as indistinct from the divine intellect, it is possible to maintain this psychology to be in close relation to Christ's Person, as do many authors.[78] Indeed, it seems very difficult to separate the ontological and psychological orders radically, such that Christ would be one Person but two independent psychological[79] subjects.[80] Spaccapelo, among others, describes Jesus as one conscious subject (Person) with two modes of consciousness:

---

in the translation above, with a double asterisk where "saltem psychologicae" stood in the original version. Pius XII, *Sempiternus Rex Christus*, 30–31; Acta Apostolicae Sedis, 43 (1951), 625–44. (Translation mine, with an eye to the Vatican translation provided in "Sempiternus Rex: Encyclical Letter of Pope Pius XII on the Fifteenth Centenary of the Council of Chalcedon," in *Collected Encyclicals of His Holiness Pope Pius XII, 1939–1954*, ed. National Catholic Welfare Conference [Washington, D.C.: Ransdell, 1954].)

78. See, e.g., Haubst, "Welche Ich?" 16–19: For Haubst, Jesus has a human "I," but this is united closely to the divine Person; it is not autonomous. Especially pertinent is 17: "Sein menschliches Ich erfuhr sich nicht nur als Ausdruck der menschlichen Natur, es erfuhr sich auch (und diese Erfahrung war vollendet in der Visio) jederzeit rückbezogen und hinbezogen auf die göttliche Hypostase, die es mitsamt der menschlichen Natur trug, und nie als von dieser verlassen."

79. This term is, of course, inapt. The psychological belongs, definitionally, to the human.

80. Spaccapelo, "Coscienza," 8: "Come … la persona é colei che compie le operazioni, così il soggetto é la stessa persona in quanto compie operazioni sensibili o razionali, cioè conscie." (The nonstandard accent marks are Spaccapelo's.) See also 14. On 24 he says the person and the subject are the same; person is ontological,

This is the solution that we accept for the problem of psychological unity: in Christ there is only one conscious *subject,* the divine Person of the Word. However, this consciousness is twofold in mode, divine and human. One and the same divine Person of the Word is divinely conscious through his divine Nature and humanly conscious through his human nature. If one keeps in minds that *who* is conscious is the person and the *mode* of this consciousness is determined by the nature, the present solution does not provide the slightest difficulty. Since consciousness is of the person and of acts, and according to the perfection of acts, and as the single Person of the Word subsists in divine and human natures, and as the single Person of the Word performs actions according to his divine and human natures, so the single Person of the Word is conscious of himself and of his acts according to his divine and human natures.[81]

Spaccapelo's formulation focuses our attention on the centrality of the personal subject in consciousness. However, that a single person could be the principle of more than one consciousness, in this sui generis case, makes us rethink one widespread understanding of personhood. We cannot understand Jesus as one subject or Person, with two ways of taking possession of his personhood, while simultaneously accepting the

while subject is psychological, but these coincide totally. Cf. Lonergan, *Constitution of Christ,* 246–47. Cf. Battaglia, "I 'Sentimenti,'" 245.

81. "[Q]uesta é la soluzione che accettiamo per il problema dell'unità psicologica: in Cristo uno solo é il *soggetto* conscio, la Persona divina del Verbo; ma tale coscienza é duplice nel modo, divino e umano. La stessa Persona divina del Verbo é divinamente conscia per la sua natura divina e umanamente conscia per la sua natura umana. Se si tiene presente che *chi* é conscio é la persona e il *modo* di tale coscienza é dato dalla natura, la presente soluzione non fa la più piccola difficoltà. Poiché la coscienza é della persona e degli atti, e secondo la perfezione degli atti, come l'unica Persona del Verbo sussiste nelle nature divina e umana, come l'unica Persona del Verbo compie operazioni secondo le nature divina e umana, così l'unica Persona del Verbo é conscia di se e dei suoi atti secondo la natura divina e secondo la natura umana"; see Spaccapelo, "Coscienza," 31. See also Lonergan, *Constitution of Christ,* 244–45.

modern identification of person and consciousness, such that to be self-conscious is strictly to be a person and vice versa.[82] We can speak of a human consciousness in Christ only if we refrain from equating this consciousness with a subject.

When the way is clear of such misunderstandings of conscious life, we can avoid the assumption that a distinct human consciousness means multiplying personal subjects or of unduly extending the autonomy and independence of his human consciousness. Philippe de la Trinité goes a step further in denying the created intellect of Christ a stand-alone consciousness, at least in rhetorical force. He argues that humanity is not the sort of reality that can be conscious, thus the problem of the human consciousness of Christ is a false problem from the beginning. He says:

> The humanity of Christ implies a consciousness [*conscience*], but IT *does not have consciousness,* because IT is not a personal subject. Only the Word of God *has,* in this nature, consciousness of living and suffering as the God-man.[83]

82. Jammarrone, *L'Unità psicologica,* 6: The modern conception of the person—accepted by Anton Günther—comes from idealism and Descartes. The person has been lately identified with self-consciousness, rather than viewed as an ontological reality. On 12–13, Jammarrone describes Vatican I's condemnation of this identification (the condemnation is nonauthoritative, he avers on 12 and 15): if person means self-consciousness, then infants would not be persons and the Trinitarian Persons would have distinct consciousnesses. Cf. 150: he argues that if there are two consciousness in Christ, then there are two persons, if we insist on an identification of person with consciousness. Cf. Cé, "Discussione," 267, note 2, and 280.

83. "L'humanité du Christ implique une conscience, mais ELLE *n'a pas conscience,* car ELLE n'est pas un sujet personnel. Seul le Verbe de Dieu *a,* en cette nature, conscience de vivre et de souffrir en homme-Dieu"; see Philippe de la Trinité, "A propos de la conscience du Christ: Une faux problème théologique," *Ephemerides Carmeliticae* 11 (1960): 3–52, 17. Christ's human nature does not have consciousness of itself, for Philippe de la Trinité, but Christ has consciousness of himself as man; on 25 he says: "Sa nature humaine n'a pas conscience d'elle-même,

It seems to be a straightforward theological requirement, implied by Christ's integral humanity, to grant that he is humanly conscious. Demurring from this admission runs against the implications of Chalcedon. To be human in an actualized state includes consciousness. His divine "consciousness" cannot be said, somewhat in style of Apollinaris of Laodicea, to supplant his human consciousness. Yet the cautions just mentioned impress upon us the need for describing this human consciousness in such a way that it is clear that Christ does not have a distinct human subjectivity. We can be successful, here again, by holding in view a defensible understanding of person and nature. Christ's human consciousness must be said to terminate in his Person, even as it is the action of this Person. If his consciousness terminates in human nature itself, that is, if his self-awareness is of a human I in acting, we cannot avoid the corrective recourse to the beatific vision mentioned earlier, in which Christ's self-impressions are transferred in knowledge (not consciousness) to their true personal subject.

## DIVIDED CONSCIOUSNESS AND SELF-UNDERSTANDING

Christ is but one divine, personal subject in his human understanding, but we cannot dissolve this understanding into his divine intellect. Does this, however, mean that his divine and human understandings are unrelated? In some perspec-

---

pas plus que mon âme, elle, n'a conscience d'appartenir à mon *Je* (comme si *elle* et *Je* étaient deux sujets distincts), mais de même que j'ai conscience de vivre de manière intelligible et sensible (en mon âme et en mon corps), de même le Verbe de Dieu a-t-Il Lui aussi conscience de vivre *en homme* (en son âme et son corps)." For contrast in Galtier's view of this issue, see Cé, "Discussione," 280.

tives, the fact of the hypostatic union does little or nothing to alter the human knowing of Christ.[84] We referred above in a general way to one fashion in which the impact of the divine Person is softened with respect to Christ's human intellection. Many theologians today propose an occlusion of the divine light from the human knowing and consciousness of Christ. Ranged among the possibilities for expressing such an occlusion is the suggestion of a partition in Christ's human intellect.

With his version of divine-occlusion theory, Jacques Maritain suggests the possibility of a growth in Christ's human understanding.[85] The vision of God is present to Christ, Maritain suggests, only as the upper region of his conscious life, the "supraconsciousness." In his supraconsciousness, Jesus is fully aware that he is God.[86] Growth in understanding happens as the lower region of consciousness, Christ's wayfaring consciousness, approximates this higher awareness in increasing

84. E.g., see Frederick E. Crowe, "The Mind of Jesus," *Communio* 1, no. 4 (1974): 365–84, 369: "[D]oes the doctrine of his divinity conflict with the supposition of a normal cognitional process in Jesus? My answer to this question would be that his divinity has nothing directly to do with it, one way or the other." Crowe exploits Lonergan's distinction between knowledge and consciousness. The experience that is Christ's self-consciousness does not carry over into an explicit self-knowledge; see 372–73, 377.

85. Maritain puts forward his explanation in Maritain, *Grace and Humanity*. Cf. Maloney, *Knowledge of Christ,* 127, 129–30, 136–37, et passim, on an area or way in which Christ has less distinct knowledge. See Jammarrone, *L'Unità psicologica,* 20–22, for a description of an early twentieth-century Christology similar to Maritain's on this point.

86. Maritain, *Grace and Humanity,* 56: The supraconsciousness of Jesus is a "consciousness" of self and is the beatific vision. "[I]t did not only show to Jesus the holy Trinity and His own divinity, it could not but show to Him also,—although not by reflection on His acts,—that His own Person, the divine Word, was the Self from which all the acts produced by His human faculties proceeded and into which led, in order to be sustained in being, all that which the external world caused them to feel or to suffer."

clarity. This growing awareness is mediated for Christ by infused knowledge.[87] Thus Maritain can say that Jesus knew the "day or hour" in his supraconsciousness, but that did not know this in his wayfaring consciousness.[88]

Karl Rahner has also put forward an explanation of Christ's consciousness that would fall loosely under the rubric of divine occlusion. Whereas Maritain describes Christ's consciousness as divided into an upper and a lower region, Rahner identifies two ways of knowing in Christ with his characteristic distinction between the subjective and transcendental, on the one hand, and the objective and categorical, on the other.[89] Christ's

87. See Maritain, *Grace and Humanity,* 104, 107–8, 116–17. On 108, perhaps in some tension with 56, he says: "To see *God* was the affair of His beatific vision; to see *that He was God,* that of his infused science." Cf. 90–91: depending on Thomas and John of St. Thomas, Maritain argues for the need for infused knowledge in Christ in addition to that of the beatific vision, so that Christ can know in a way proportioned to the human mind. Yet, on 94 et passim he makes it clear that infused knowledge stands on the higher side of the partition between the supraconsciousness and the lower consciousness and is "strictly *incommunicable.*" Pages 94–95 suggest that the agent intellect formulates concepts to concretize and express the truth held by infused knowledge. Cf. 103, where infused knowledge provides expression of the beatific vision. On 114, Jesus knew who he was from infused knowledge before he could express it to himself by concepts. Cf. further 59–60 and 72–73. Alexandre Durand, in "Science du Christ," 501, points out that beatific knowledge is incommunicable. On this point in connection with infused knowledge, cf. also White, "Voluntary Action," 515–17, 519, and Torrell, "S. Thomas d'Aquin et la science du Christ," 396–97 and 403 (which should be taken in the context of the whole article). A few authors find an incommunicability and/or indistinctness of Christ's knowledge and compare this to mystical experience in the saints. Among them are: Torrell, "S. Thomas d'Aquin et la science," 400; Durand, "Science du Christ," 500–501; Crowe, "Mind of Jesus," 372, 381–82; and Mongeau, "Human and Divine Knowing," 38–39. Cf. Haubst, "Welche Ich?" 11.

88. Maritain, *Grace and Humanity,* 96. Alexandre Durand, in "Science du Christ," 502, argues that Christ's lower consciousness does not have direct access to the upper and its content.

89. Rahner develops these ideas in Rahner, "Dogmatic Reflections." Cf. Duquoc, *Christologie,* 154, 157–58, 162–63: Duquoc argues that because there is a

nescience of certain facts and phenomena, at least on an explicit level, is not a liability but, rather, finds a positive place in Rahner's theology.[90] This nescience gradually gives way, however, to an increasingly articulate self-understanding. Rahner suggests that that which is known to Christ, unthematically and as subjectively foundational, gradually becomes crystallized in Christ's objective self-reflection. Rahner's treatment of this problem locates the vision of God within the hypostatic union, instead of requiring the vision to serve as Christ's objective notification that he is hypostatically united as man to the Word.[91]

In view of common experience, the idea of a mental partition, as we find in Maritain, or of a distinction between objective knowing and subjective coknowing, as we find in Rahner, is an entirely alluring solution. We cannot deny that we have awarenesses and insights above the reach of our explicit knowledge and vision of reality. In his well-known discussion of the memory in the *Confessions,* Augustine gives an example of searching for something, such as a name, and in the process dismissing all suggestions that do not match that which is implicitly known and inexpressible.[92] Everyone has had the inde-

---

distinction between consciousness and knowledge, it is possible to say that Christ lacks knowledge without implying that he is not God.

90. Cf. Pannenberg, *Jesus—God and Man,* 332–34. Cf. also Erich Fascher, "'Von dem Tage aber und von der Stunde weiß niemand ...'": Der Anstoß in Mark. 13, 32 (Matth. 24, 36)—Eine exegetische Skizze zum Verhältnis von historisch-kritischer und christologischer Interpretation," in *Ruf und Antwort: Festgabe für Emil Fuchs zum 90. Geburtstag* (Leipzig: Koehler & Amelang, 1964), 482–83, which suggests salvific relevance in nescience.

91. Cf. Amato, *Gesù il signore,* 395–96. Cf. the argument in Mansini, "Understanding St. Thomas," 92–95, to the effect that hypostatic union does not strictly imply the vision of God in St. Thomas's thought.

92. Augustine, *Confessions,* trans. Henry Chadwick (New York: Oxford University Press, 1991), 195–196; book 10, 18/27–19/28.

scribable, "anamnetic" experience of coming to realize what he or she, in a different sense, knew already.

Although everyone can identify with this or a similar experience, a separate question is whether it applies to the beatific vision. The beatific vision is nonconceptual and (for all of the difference between Rahner's and Maritain's explanations) unthematic and supraconscious experience is nonconceptual, but there is an important difference between these two. Beatific knowledge is only incidentally connected to conceptualization, and this only in the very particular case of the God-man who reveals that which he receives from the Father in concepts intelligible to human beings. Unthematic awareness of the horizon of being and supraconsciousness as Maritain describes it are both essentially related to the conceptual order either as condition or prelude to concepts. In different ways we can call both unthematic and supraconscious knowledge "preconceptual." Beatific knowledge is not preconceptual; rather, it has the character of an endpoint. Preconceptual understanding is intrinsically indistinct because it is for conceptualization. In other words, it forms part of the activity of the mind that produces concepts by which understanding occurs. If the indistinctness that plays an essential role in intramundane reasoning is linked to the immediate vision of God, one gets the impression that the discussion is misplaced. When we set aside the ordinary, conceptualizing work of the mind, that is, when the mind is passive as is the case with the beatific vision, is there still room to talk about intelligibility that is not fully or directly present? When concepts are "off the table," does a distinction between thematic and unthematic knowing, or one between conscious and supraconscious, still have a place?

Perhaps, however, questions regarding the will paradoxically outweigh epistemological considerations in this matter of the intellect. Is it humanly possible to make an act of the will with respect to implicit awarenesses and insights above our cognizance? However much these influence our (fully) conscious decisions, we do not decide for or on them. We cannot confuse the effects of a supraconscious or prethematic "understanding" with acts of the will as such. We will see momentarily that the reach of this problem is increased as we bring into view the fact that the acts of the will here in question are acts of supreme love.

Furthermore, not all theologians have been content to divide Christ's human knowledge into more or less discrete spheres (even if the question of the Magisterium could be shown to have no bearing on this issue).[93] Gutwenger, for example, writes:

> The attempt to divide the human soul of Christ into different regions in order to house contradictory spiritual experiences is ... hardly acceptable. For consciousness is an undivided and homogeneous factor, at least insofar as a definite conscious experience necessarily excludes its opposite from the psychological point of view when it reaches a certain intensity. If we prefer to ignore this fact we run the risk of implying more than one *ego*.[94]

93. Cf. Alexandre Durand, who in "Science du Christ," 499–500, indicates the possibility of seeing the knowledge of Christ as total on one plane, in stated fidelity to the Holy Office's 1918 intervention, and to see limited knowledge on another plane. Cf. also Rahner, "Dogmatic Reflections," 199, 204, and 213.

94. Gutwenger, "Christ's Knowledge," 92. Cf. Maloney, *Knowledge of Christ,*

If Gutwenger is correct that these theologies risk a plurality of egos, then in the same stroke they undercut Jesus' mission in the world as the one Mediator between God and man.[95] At first blush it does not seem as though these ideas bear any significant connection to each other. Why is it appropriate for Christ to have a single subjectivity with a clear human consciousness in order to save the world? In the next and final section of this chapter, we will bring to the fore the soteriological considerations that have implicitly motivated our discussion so far.

## SOTERIOLOGY

If salvation is only a divine act, we can readily agree that there is no thoughtful, human component to it. God reminds Job that he does many things without human knowledge or cooperation. We must earnestly put to ourselves the question of whether the Redemption is this sort of action. If it is—if we are comfortable with a soteriology that, even without wanting to, makes of Christ's humanity an unwitting passenger in the trajectory toward a Cross that is borne precisely in this humanity itself—then we do not need to tax ourselves with the issue of Christ's knowledge. If, on the other hand, we find this understanding of redemption unacceptable, then we are faced with questions pertaining to the human understanding of Christ on two fronts. Jesus has knowledge of those he redeems as well as self-understanding. We must grant that

35: "[D]ivinity implies consciousness. The notion of divinity in a state of suspended consciousness is an impossible one in the Judeo-Christian tradition about God."

95. 1 Tm 2:5.

there is a basic difference between knowledge and consciousness of oneself and knowledge of others. However, these two forms of knowledge cannot be seen in independence of each other. Christ's knowledge of others must be rooted in and informed by his self-consciousness. From the other side, his self-understanding in turn is conditioned in some way by his knowledge of those he was sent to redeem, as we will see more fully in the next chapter in connection with Maurice Blondel's thought. We can let go of neither end of the rope if we are to make sense of salvation. If Christ knows others but has no true knowledge of himself, he is deluded and he is less than those he was sent to redeem.[96] If he knows himself but not others, it becomes difficult to understand that he is the Savior.

We do not have to entertain any form of Gnosticism to hold that knowledge is essential to Christ's mission. Christ's personal love on earth (reflected in the "for me" of Gal 2:20) has been recalled in connection with his knowledge, in some form, of individual people.[97] St. Thomas and Pope Pius XII, among others, link his human knowledge to salvation.[98] Yet it

96. Rahner, "Dogmatic Reflections," 206, and, among other texts, Jean Mouroux, "Maurice Blondel et la conscience du Christ," in *L'Homme devant Dieu: Mélanges offerts au Père Henri de Lubac* (Paris: Aubier, 1964), 194.

97. Maloney, *Knowledge of Christ,* 123–24. Maloney signals the 1985 International Theological Commission's citation of Gal 2:20 to this effect, in *The Consciousness of Christ Concerning Himself and His Mission.* Innumerable authors have been helpful in pointing to an essential connection between Christ's knowledge and the accomplishment of his mission.

98. *ST* 3, 14, 4 and Pius XII, *Mystici corporis,* 75; DS 3812: "[V]ero amantissima cognitio, qua divinus Redemptor a primo Incarnationis suae momento nos prosecutus est, studiosam quamlibet humanae mentis vim exsuperat; quandoquidem per beatam illam visionem, qua vixdum in Deiparae sinu exceptus, fruebatur, omnia mystici Corporis membra continenter perpetuoque sibi praesentia habet, suoque complectitur salutifero amore."

is not easy to see in what way we can substantiate these ideas. Léopold Malevez, in an article indicated by Hans Urs von Balthasar, draws an important connection between the human knowledge of Christ and salvation.[99] In this article, Malevez seeks to show that Christ's personal presence to everyone can be defended from an Aristotelian/Thomistic perspective.[100] Form, although passive in one regard, has a dynamic and virtual élan. It would seek to replicate itself because of its unlimitedness, but it cannot numerically and literally do so. This dynamism is thus directed within the self instead.[101] It implies a presence to every other instantiation of the same form. There is a latent presence of every human in each human.

> All possible states of humanity are prefigured in each of us and reside there as latent virtualities. What, in effect, is the present limitlessness of our form and the fullness of its being but the unison of the real and possible activities originated by the human race, the totality of those corporeal, intellectual and moral events to which humanity continually gives birth in its indefinite proliferation: the innocence of the child and the tenderness of mothers, literary knowledge and the courage of the martyr? Being virtually infinite in each of us, the human form is, by that fact, virtually all of these things. No doubt, this form is individualized in us by matter. This means that it is presently constricted to a partial and strictly defined expression: it cannot be simultaneously the candor of a child and the subtle irony of a sage. Potentially and dynamically, however, the

99. Hans Urs von Balthasar, *Theo-Drama: Theological Dramatic Theory,* trans. Graham Harrison, vol. 3, *Dramatis Personae: Persons in Christ* (San Francisco: Ignatius Press, 1992), 233, note 6.

100. Léopold Malevez, S.J., "L'Église dans le Christ, II," *Recherches de Science religieuse* 25 (1935): 418–40.

101. Malevez, "L'Église," 431–32.

form, once again, recounts in each individual the whole history of the human race and precontains its entire future.[102]

The presence of each to others here is merely potential.[103] However, according to Malevez, a full ecclesiology would require a presence or mutual containment of human persons that is actual. This could be realized within a Thomistic framework by the all-encompassing knowledge of Christ.[104]

Jesus redeems those whom he actually possesses in himself in knowledge. The human knowledge of Christ is not, then, just an adornment of his human nature or perfection that is due to the grace of union, although it is true that union implies such perfection.[105] Rather, there is a soteriological import to his knowing. Malevez says:

This perfect knowledge [*connaissance*], this way of having had everything that we are in thought and in affection, this "heart" of Christ occupies a privileged place in the economy of redemption. By means of this, in effect, we can begin to understand why the

102. "[T]ous les états possibles de l'humanité sont préfigurés en chacun de nous et y demeurent à la manière de virtualités latentes. Qu'est-ce, en effet, que l'illimitation actuelle de notre forme et la plénitude de son être, sinon l'ensemble des activités réelles ou possibles développées par notre espèce, la totalité des événements corporels, intellectuels et moraux auxquels l'humanité donne successivement le jour dans sa prolifération indéfinie: l'innocence de l'enfant et la tendresse des mères, la science du lettré et la vaillance du martyr? La forme humaine, étant, en chacun de nous, virtuellement infinie, est, par là même, virtuellement tout cela; certes, se trouvant en nous individuée par une matière, elle est, conséquemment, contrainte 'actuellement' à une expression partielle et strictement définie: elle ne peut être à la fois et la candeur de l'enfant et la fine ironie du sage, mais potentiellement, et même dynamiquement, la forme, encore une fois, raconte en chaque individu toute l'histoire de l'espèce et précontient tout son avenir"; see Malevez, "L'Église," 430.

103. Malevez, "L'Église," 436.

104. Malevez, "L'Église," 437.

105. Malevez, "L'Église," 438–39.

Father—with ourselves being present in the love and consciousness [*conscience*] of the God-man—was able to accept, without the slightest fiction, the satisfaction and merit of Jesus Christ as an act of the whole human race.[106]

Perhaps we are hesitant to follow Malevez in every detail. Yet, if the main lines of his point are taken seriously, we cannot be content with a theology that leaves the merit of the Redemption with a voluntarist's surmise that redemption works as it does because God has ordained that it so works. We will look more closely at the idea of merit and the Cross in the next two chapters, but several points should be signaled here by way of rooting Christ's knowledge, as promised, in his mission. We must at least try to find an intrinsic, not merely arbitrary, link that binds Jesus' full, human knowing to salvation.[107]

In the first place, we should hold fast to the idea that the Cross is the supreme human act of love and accept as true whatever this really implies. We would find ourselves some-

106. "[C]ette connaissance parfaite, cette manière d'avoir été tout ce que nous sommes, par la pensée et la sympathie, ce 'coeur' du Christ occuperait une place de premier plan dans l'économie rédemptrice; par là, en effet, peut-être commencerions-nous à comprendre pourquoi le Père, nous trouvant présents dans l'amour et dans la conscience de l'Homme-Dieu, a pu, sans aucune fiction, accepter la satisfaction et le mérite de Jésus-Christ comme l'acte du genre humain tout entier"; see Léopold Malevez, "L'Église," 439.

107. Cf. John P. Galvin, "From the Humanity of Christ to the Jesus of History: A Paradigm Shift in Catholic Christology," *Theological Studies* 55 (1994): 252–73, 255–66, 268–69. I cannot claim that Fr. Galvin's broad comments regarding Jesus' conscious freedom in the act of salvation and awareness of his own identity as the Christ endorse the claims that I make here, but his remarks have some bearing on the present discussion: "[T]o conceive of a decisive salvific figure who remains unaware of such personal significance is to reduce the mediation of salvation to a subpersonal level." Cf. also John P. Galvin, "The Death of Jesus in Contemporary Theology: Systematic Perspectives and Historical Issues," *Horizons* 13, no. 2 (1986): 239–52, 245–48, 252.

what pressed in making this claim if the Cross were characterized by indefinition and anonymity. How could the Cross contain within itself every true and supernatural act of personal love if it were somehow vaguer than these? The Cross, to illustrate, is the sustaining condition of martyrdom, but the martyr well knows for whom he or she is dying. Love in the human order is predicated on knowing.[108] God's knowledge of things is inseparable from the fact that he has loved them into existence.[109] His love is prior to our knowledge of things as they exist in themselves. For us, the "order" of human knowing and loving is reversed: intelligibility does not flow from love; it flows into love. Christ loves as a man and he loves as God. He loves with the creative love that underpins knowledge while, from the other direction, he humanly loves that which he knows. Christ is the fulcrum for a pincer movement of creation and re-creation.

Furthermore, if we continue to sift through the elements of human love and try to follow these as they indicate to us something in the way Christ knows, we see on an experiential plane that loves are as different as the people to whom they are directed. There is no need to call into question the fact that human persons stand under a common universal in order to grant that human persons are not defined wholly with reference to the species. There is not much more to say about a particular squirrel than that it is a squirrel, but the idea of Paul is not exhausted by the mere affirmation that Paul is a man. Personal love has a correspondingly incomparable character. It

108. *ST* 1, 82, 4.
109. *ST* 1, 20, 2.

is not that there is no gradation in love or lovability, but love cannot be defined only with respect to rank in an otherwise homogeneous series. The more perfect things are, the less they admit of simple comparison to each other. If a child were to ask her father which sibling he loved the most, the question—straightforward enough—would somehow come across as incomprehensible. A father does not typically have to make an effort to love each of his children equally; rather, since he loves his children not simply as examples in a category (e.g., one's offspring), he loves each with a love that is incommensurable with any other love he bears. There is no comparison, in one sense, with the loves that correspond to persons precisely because comparisons are of relatively little value in the case of persons. It would be strange not to apply this very basic fact of human experience to redemption. The Christ of Galatians did not redeem Paul because Paul happened to have the ticket of being human. He did not redeem Paul because Paul was the member of a class of beings that Christ generically pictured in connection with his sacrificial action and that he took with himself to the Cross. He loved Paul as Paul.[110] Human persons are not redeemed in the same way that they qualify for tax exemptions.

110. Cf. Matthew Levering, *Christ's Fulfillment of Torah and Temple: Salvation According to Thomas Aquinas* (Notre Dame, Ind.: University of Notre Dame Press, 2002), 39–40: "By possessing the fullness of knowing and loving, [Christ] is able to *know* each person in light of God's plan for the salvation of all, and he is able to *love* each person who is included in God's plan for the salvation of all. Thus he does not need to wait to meet us in heaven before knowing and loving us; his personal love for each of us is given, in St. Paul's phrase, while we are still in our sins. In short, Christ's establishment in beatitude, far from making him an ahistorical figure, actually enables him, precisely in his historical life, to perform the historical work of salvation in the personal way that it must be performed."

A beneficent act of will that is not specific and personal is not love in the full sense; it is a dispensation. While we have to be on guard against prooftexting Jesus' indications in Jn 10 that he knows his sheep intimately, even by name, there is no harm in admitting that these verses point to the intimate and personal love that Christ, even on earth, bears for his own. In chapter 2 we will continue to seek a description of the embracing understanding on which redeeming love is founded in order to anchor our reflections in chapter 3 on the love or volitional activity itself by which Jesus redeems. Before elaborating these ideas, we cannot fail to confront the question of whether or not the knowledge described here is realistic.[111] To suggest that such a comprehensive knowledge would be *ideal* with respect to Christ's voluntary life and salvific mission is not yet to show that it is *possible.* For a variety of reasons, today's thought world has shaded this question with a particular difficulty even as it has leant a special urgency to its answer.

The Savior of the human world humanly knows the world that he saves. This claim is a tall order. Christ here seems to know too much to be truly human. Such an impression comes to us readily enough, but is it a valid conclusion? Are there prescribed limits on human understanding outside of which a mind can no longer be considered human? Have we determined a particular finite point, to the exclusion of other finite points, at which mental capaciousness cannot be imagined ex-

111. Thomas G. Weinandy, in "Jesus' Filial Vision," 198–99, also suggests the importance of Christ's having humanly known those he redeemed, while acknowledging mystery in the manner of this knowing. On the soteriological importance of Christ's knowledge in general, Mansini, "Understanding St. Thomas," 106–10, is insightful and lucid.

cept in contradiction to humanity? No one can deny that a human mind must be finite; but the implication that we can and must be more specific than this stems in some measure from a visceral, rather than a reasoned, conviction.

Often when such an objection to full human knowledge is adduced, it is so to the effect that Christ would not have experienced human life *as* we experience it. But how far are we willing to push this line of thinking? Does any human person experience the human condition in the very way that any other person does? Is there a preestablished tolerable range of difference between one's own life experience and that of Christ in deference to which we can safely grant that he really entered into the human condition? We must proceed in extreme caution when we are tempted to assign limits, strictures, and conditions to being human. Many of history's tragedies have been played out on the stage of such pat conclusions.

We must add to this an important consideration. For all the intellectual capacity that we might assign to Christ in his humanity, it remains the case that his human knowing is *infinitesimal* in comparison with his divine understanding. As such, the comparison of Christ's intellect to ours is of relatively little moment. Both ordinary human minds and Christ's human mind fall infinitely short of infinite capacity. Although, from our common perspective, the difference between our thinking and Christ's thinking as suggested here can seem overwhelming, ours stands as immeasurably more like, than unlike, that of Christ.

Instead of trying to find the point at which we begin to feel disquieted by intellectual operations and achievements accorded to Christ—and assigning to this point a kind of cognitive maximum in his human life—we must, again, ask whether a relatively comprehensive and profound understanding is humanly possible and—if it is—in what terms we can conceive of it.

It is probably true that few Christians find themselves particularly troubled by the assumption that, in Heaven, people will enjoy an abundant and overflowing knowledge, not just of God but also of other realities in God. For what reason is acceptance of a plenitude of knowledge in the saints not extended in some form to Christ? Perhaps it is Christ's being on earth that is an obstacle. This may be the case partly for the fact that Christ's humanity did not then enjoy the full overflowing of his glory—which condition seems the more important the less one reflects on it—and partly for the fact that his time on earth was limited, even brief. In light of the latter fact, we are apt to puzzle over the reality that thoughts ordinarily take time and, if we reckon as Paul seems to have done that Jesus somehow knows specific people, we would be inclined to require that Christ think about such people serially and specifically. Yet, if each thought is serial, discrete, and takes a given amount of time—no matter how small we reasonably imagine this time to be—then Jesus does not have the time on earth to think of billions of people.

We must question the assumptions here. Is all human knowing accounted for by the paradigm of discursive processing? We must certainly relax this model in the case of beatific knowing, which, moreover, we should not imagine to occupy mental "space" in the same way that discursive knowing based on sensible experience does. Beatific knowing does not employ species or images.[112] This is not, of course, to insist that beatific knowing could not yield resonances with corporeal imagery and other thought processes. In itself, however, the model of beatific knowing requires that the questions concerning the "space" in Christ's mind and the time needed to achieve thoughts that correspond to specific realities (like human persons) be asked in a different way. In this we begin to see from another perspective how important the traditional notion of Christ's beatific knowledge on earth is to soteriological concerns.

Is there not, however, a fundamental problem in holding that physical, sensible realities—as human beings are—can be understood without a necessarily discursive recourse to sensible representations? If human persons are individuated by matter, are not phantasms, in which material particularity is registered, absolutely required for knowing? In response to these questions we must observe that to know *that* a particular person is individualized by such-and-such features is not exactly and necessarily equivalent to mentally conjuring up these features every time this person's name is mentioned. On recognition of a person's name, there is no doubt in the knower's mind about that person's identity, although the knower may not always pause to represent for himself or herself the known person's features, that is, he or she achieves identification without representation. We do this quite ordinarily with numbers and distances, to give only two more examples. When I must deal in the number 15, I do not (now) try to picture fifteen apples on a table. When I surmise that it is eight

112. Cessario, "Incarnate Wisdom," 338. Cf. Levering, *Christ's Fulfillment,* 59–60.

more miles to home, I do not strain to imagine the span of twelve inches 42,240 times on end. Not all knowing of sensible things is linked to sensible representation.[113]

Perhaps, finally, it will be easier to acknowledge a knowing in Christ that is both extensive and unfettered by the labors of processing if we recall that classical epistemology is not uncomfortable with the notion of metacorporeal thinking. It is not necessary to rearticulate or differentiate classical theories of cognition here; it suffices to signal that traditional notions of knowing did not see the soul in its understanding as strictly limited to brain activity and classical theorists maintained this understanding without in any way succumbing to the temptations that would later absorb the attention of Cartesians and their (oftentimes materialist) opponents. St. Thomas, for example, marshaled reasons to think that understanding could not, in principle, be limited to a corporeal organ.[114] Of course, Thomas's intent was hardly to rule out the rational soul's self-expressive employment of the body (with the brain) as the body's form. However, his understanding of this relationship in its emphasis on the dispositive engagement of (corporeally "located") phantasms meant that the intellect's dependence

113. We have analogies for this in God's knowing and in that of angels. Cf. Jean-Louis Chrétien, *Le regard de l'amour* (Paris: Desclée de Brouwer, 2000), 137–38: "L'ange n'a pas besoin de rencontrer pour connaître: sa connaissance n'est pas la perpétuelle *épreuve,* en tous les sens du terme, que constitue la nôtre." For a worthwhile treatment of angelic knowledge in general, see 125–39. See also *ST* 1, 57, 2 and 1, 55, 3 ad 3m. The case of separated souls' knowledge, even of corporeal realities, which St. Thomas takes up in Question 89 of the *Prima pars,* sheds even more light on the present issue. On knowing in general without imagining phantasms, see *Summa contra gentiles,* 1, 55, 4.

114. See, e.g., *ST* 1 75, 2; 1, 76, 1 and 1, 84, 7.

on the body could never be seen as absolute.[115] Although strictly philosophical, this notion enjoyed the advantage that it could be reconciled with the doctrinal affirmation that separated souls truly know God.[116] If brain activity is coterminous in every way with intellection, an intermediate state is impossible. This claim clearly defies neuroreductive approaches to the so-called mind-body problem, but such approaches have notably failed to gain consensus within scientific and philosophical fora.[117]

We should not be surprised if at this point we find ourselves back where we started: at the claim that Jesus possessed the beatific vision while on earth. Jesus' human knowledge of particular human beings is principally grounded in this, rather

115. See *ST* 1, 89, 5.

116. Cf. Benedict XII's *Benedictus Deus,* DS 1305.

117. For the sake of space, no comprehensive list of helpful sources pertaining to the mind-body debate can be given here. One outstanding contribution, however, should be mentioned. M. R. Hacker and P. M. S. Bennett, *Philosophical Foundations of Neuroscience* (Malden, Mass., Oxford, U.K., and Carlton, Victoria, Australia: Blackwell, 2003) identifies a conceptual problem in positions that reduce cognition to brain activity; there is a strong resonance of this criticism with the concerns of traditional philosophy. See, e.g., 3: "The ascription of psychological—in particular, cognitive and cogitative—attributes to the brain is ... a source of much ... confusion. Neuroscience can investigate the neural conditions and concomitants of the acquisition, possession and exercise of sentient powers by animals. It can discover the neural preconditions for the possibility of the exercise of distinctly human powers of thought and reasoning, of articulate memory and imagination, of emotion and volition. This it can do by patient inductive correlation between neural phenomena and the possession and exercise of psychological powers, and between neural damage and deficiencies in normal mental function. What it *cannot* do is *replace* the wide range of ordinary psychological explanations of human activities in terms of reasons, intentions, purposes, goals, values, rules and conventions by neurological explanations.... It is the animal that perceives, not parts of its brain, and it is human beings who think and reason, not their brains. The brain and its activities *make it possible* for *us*—not for *it*—to perceive and think, to feel emotions, and to form and pursue projects."

than in the other modes of his knowing: experience and the infusion of species. Christ was possessed of and really used the "ordinary," discursive, phantastic mode of human knowing, but given the true spatial and temporal constraints of Jesus' time on earth, we cannot locate his knowledge of all particular human persons in his experiential knowledge. Infused knowledge (of universals) would only provide the particular knowledge that we are looking for here either on the assumption that particulars are contained as particulars in the universal—which some authors maintain—or on the assumption that the human mind can deduct intuitively.[118] The latter assumption warrants a closer look. In the case of an angel, God's revelation of his creative will is said to qualify the species possessed in infused knowledge such that real, concrete existents are known. This "process" is atemporal (aeviternal) in an angel. It is only with some difficulty, however, that we can think of progress from the general to the particular as atemporal or as taking little time in a human person, since the human person accomplishes this move, that is, deducts, in a ratiocinative, rather than an intuitive, movement.

In the traditional terminology, we say that Jesus sees human persons as secondary objects of the beatific vision.[119] This is of more than passing significance, since to see human beings in God is to see them in their fullest clarity and in the source of

118. Despite the terminology used here, Duns Scotus's understanding of intuitive knowledge is an unrelated issue.

119. Randall S. Rosenberg, in "Christ's Human Knowledge: A Conversation with Lonergan and Balthasar," *Theological Studies* 71 (2010): 817–45, 834–35, clarifies how this has been understood by Lonergan and his followers. See also Maloney, "The Mind of Christ," 292–95.

their most profound meaning. This is not to say that every human or angelic person that Jesus humanly sees in this way must be saved, but it does suggest that, in seeing in God the end-point of those who reach God, Jesus is intimately aware, as the human Son of God, of his Father's plan for reaching that end.

[ 2 ]

# THE CHRISTOLOGY OF MAURICE BLONDEL AND SACRED HEART DEVOTION

## INTRODUCTION

Even those who would be sympathetic to Maurice Blondel's high Christology would find it incomplete and unsatisfactory.[1] He cannot be faulted, however, for having left certain aspects of his thought here open-ended and unclarified. Not least in weight of the reasons for exculpating Blondel for his

This chapter originally appeared as an article in *Gregorianum* in 2007; it is reprinted here by the kind permission of the editor. I have made only minor emendations to the original text, such as translating quotations appearing in the text body and changing quotation marks and notes to conform to the style used elsewhere in this book.

1. Cf. Xavier Tilliette, "Is a Philosophical Christology Possible?" in *Problems and Perspectives of Fundamental Theology,* ed. René Latourelle and Gerald O'Collins, trans. Matthew O'Connell (New York and Ramsey, N.J.: Paulist Press, 1982), 149–50.

vagueness in describing Christ, the nearly invisible yet guiding endpoint of his thought,[2] is the fact that he never intended to be a theologian.[3] His Christological achievement is all the more impressive for this fact.

Blondel's Christology is decidedly and unapologetically "descending."[4] Blondel does not dim the splendor and totalizing character of the Word in order to make room for his *kenosis*; Christ is rather totalizing precisely in his *kenosis* and an account of his majesty that would sacrifice, for example, divine self-awareness is unthinkable. In order truly to invest human persons with his power and saving presence, so that he himself may be all in all, Christ seeks to embrace human reality at its depths in an experiential way. It is clear for Blondel that Christ's descent exists for the integration of human experience; humiliation serves Christ's appropriation and experience of our condition. Christ's totalizing character depends on his descent to encounter even the bitterest depths of human life.

Is Christ, however, also totalizing in his glory? It goes with-

2. See Christoph Theobald, "La Christologie transcendentale dans 'L'Action' (1893) de Maurice Blondel," *Recherches de Science religieuse* 81, no. 3 (1993): 421–58, 426, and Tilliette, "Philosophical Christology," 149.

3. Cf. René Virgoulay, "La christologie blondélienne dans la crise moderniste," in *Le Christ de Maurice Blondel,* ed. René Virgoulay (Paris: Desclée, 2003), 84: "[L]'on ne trouve pas chez Blondel de réflexion approfondie sur la Résurrection comme mystère de salut.... Certes il n'avait pas l'intention de faire une dogmatique." Regarding Christ's Easter exaltation, Virgoulay also says, "cet aspect est assez peu marqué chez Blondel." See René Virgoulay, "Postface," in *Le Christ de Maurice Blondel,* ed. René Virgoulay (Paris: Desclée, 2003), 206.

4. See, e.g., Xavier Tilliette, "Maurice Blondel et la controverse christologique," in *Le Modernisme,* ed. Pierre Colin and Dominique Dubarle (Paris: Editions Beauchesne, 1980), 156 et passim. Cf. Pierre de Cointet, "Le Médiateur: La Trilogie et La Philosophie et l'Esprit Chrétien," in *Le Christ de Maurice Blondel,* ed. René Virgoulay (Paris: Desclée, 2003), 159 et passim.

out saying for every Christian that he must be, yet Blondel only hints in this direction. If at the heart of Christ's humiliation is an embracing of everything truly human, should we expect to see the same pattern of integration in Christ's glorification? Sin is reckoned with in the embracing of the humanity that sin damages—Christ takes on the pain to humanity that sin brings; following on this, the question of how human sin would be overcome in Christ's glorification for Blondel must be examined as well. Again, this is underdeveloped in Blondel's understanding, yet we should not think of a development along these lines as foreign to the philosopher's thought but rather as potentially complementary.[5] Blondel certainly indicates Christ's passivity in the face of all experience, including sin, as we will see. I will try to show that this passivity, especially in the face of sin, should not be conceived of statically but as one moment in a diachronically understood drama of redemption. The aim of this chapter, then, is to suggest something of the *reditus* latently present in Blondel's Christological *exitus*.

In this chapter I do not intend to contribute toward an answer to the suffering-of-God question, at least in a direct way, or to describe with any sort of completeness and competence popular devotion to the Sacred Heart (which theme will appear in this chapter as a kind of test case), or, finally, to detail sufficiently Maurice Blondel's "Panchristism." However, in tying together threads from each of these areas, I hope that some-

5. Though its particular features fall somewhat to the side of our discussion here, Pierre de Cointet, in "Le Médiateur," 162–70, provides a useful summary of Blondel's notion of the Redeemer put forward in *La Philosophie et l'Esprit chrétien.*

thing profitable is returned to each. We must begin with this last mentioned, at the top, in order eventually to make our return there.

## PANCHRISTISM: CHRIST AS THE *VINCULUM SUBSTANTIALE*

Blondel[6] stands squarely in the spirit of a certain integralism, in the notion that wholeness subsists only in Christ Incarnate,[7] as well as—and this is really the same thing—in the spirit of a maximalism. He says, "Having always been a *maximist* I was deeply gratified to see the efforts of the *minimists* rebuffed. The parting of the ways has been reached, and we

6. Blondel would develop the idea that seized him from his youth. Cf. Maurice Blondel, *Carnets intimes,* vol. 1 (1883–1894) (Paris: Les Éditions du Cerf, 1961), 44: "Le *Vinculum* . . . je désigne par ce mot l'idée qui me hante toujours."

Valuable studies pertaining to Blondel's Christology, especially his Panchristism, which have contributed to the present chapter, may be found in J. W. Sullivan, "Matter for Heaven: Blondel, Christ and Creation," *Ephemerides Theologicae Lovanienses* 64, no. 1 (1988): 60–83; A. E. van Hooff, "Panchristismus: Bezugspunkt von Blondels l'Action," *Zeitschrift für Katholische Theologie* 109, no. 4 (1987): 416–30; René Virgoulay, "Exégèse, théologie et philosophie dans la réflexion christologique," *Recherches de Science religieuse* 88, no. 4 (2000): 561–78, esp. 568–69; Tilliette, "Maurice Blondel et la controverse christologique" and "Philosophical Christology," esp. 149–50; Mouroux, "Maurice Blondel et la conscience du Christ," in L'Homme devant Dieu: Mélanges offerts au Père Henri de Lubac (Paris: Aubier, 1964), esp. 190–92; and Theobald, "Christologie transcendentale." See also Maurice Blondel and Auguste Valensin, *Correspondance (1899–1912): Maurice Blondel et Auguste Valensin,* vol. 1 (Paris: Aubier, Éditions Montaigne, 1957), 43–48. Henri de Lubac has compiled and commented on a number of Blondel's texts and secondary sources regarding his Panchristism. Additionally, Pierre de Cointet, in "Le Médiateur," profitably investigates Blondel's Panchristism. Not to be overlooked for appreciating the import of Blondel's Panchristism for his thought is, finally, Xavier Tilliette, "Le panchristisme dans L'Action et les premiers écrits," in *Le Christ de Maurice Blondel,* ed. René Virgoulay (Paris: Desclée, 2003), 35–57.

7. Henri de Lubac, S.J., ed., *Pierre Teilhard de Chardin, Maurice Blondel: Correspondence,* trans. William Whitman (New York: Herder & Herder, 1967), 62.

are led to the instauratio tota in Christo: de Christo nunquam satis."[8] It is in this light that we must understand Blondel's vision of Christ.

Employing the term "Panchristism," which he would later reject as misleading,[9] Blondel sought to clarify his totalizing vision of Christ in both creation and re-creation.[10] In view of the fact that the last two generations of scholarship have yielded several fine studies of Blondel's "*panchristisme*," I will limit my description of this point and focus chiefly on the Word's glory vis-à-vis the world and his descent into human life in order to redeem it.

Early in Blondel's career he was impressed, through Leibniz, by the need for a principle to constitute and unite the individual components of reality. For the multiplicity of in-

8. De Lubac, *Chardin, Blondel,* 23. Blondel is quoted in this essay in English whenever possible. I rely on the reader's patience, however, with numerous French citations, which, due to the paucity of translations of Blondel literature into English, are unavoidable. See also Virgoulay, "Exégèse, théologie et philosophie," 567–68.

9. Blondel distanced himself from the label "Panchristism," though not from the idea itself. See de Lubac, *Chardin, Blondel,* 58–59; Sullivan, "Blondel, Christ and Creation," 77, 78; Virgoulay, "Exégèse, théologie et philosophie," 568; and Marie-Jeanne Coutagne, "Le Christ et l'énigme du monde: La christologie blondélienne 1916–1925," in *Le Christ de Maurice Blondel,* ed. René Virgoulay (Paris: Desclée, 2003), 87, 113.

10. See Blondel, *Carnets intimes,* 1:222: "Par l'Incarnation, le monde a été comme créé à nouveau; mais d'une manière transcendante et idéale." Cf. Virgoulay, "Exégèse, théologie et philosophie," 568. As an aside, it is noteworthy that Blondel also favors an ecclesial "maximalism." As Christ is totalizing, so will his Church be: "Catholicism is nothing if it is not everything. Its very name would be a lie if anything at all escaped its design, the only one intended by God's providence. This means that we must reject absolutely the widespread notion of a religion that would have its moments of glory or its restricted domain but would not permeate the whole atmosphere we breathe and all the forms of our activity"; see Maurice Blondel, "Philosophy Fulfilled in Christianity," in *Christian Witness in the Secular City,* ed. Everett Morgan (Chicago: Loyola University Press, 1970), 89.

dividual things to be established as a whole there is necessary, for Blondel, a principle that grounds this whole in transcending it.[11] God actively undertakes a passion in creating—activity alone on God's part would not effect things as constituents of a whole.[12] Rather, in addition to creating with an effective will, God unites them in the passive, yet integrating, perception of them as real.

> [A] rational and productive knowledge [is not] enough; there has to be a perceptive and passive knowledge. The reality of things consists in mediating between this double aspect. They are, then, on the condition that their multiple heterogeneity acts on whoever perceives and undergoes them; they are, on the condition that these multiple and passive perceptions, reduced to the unity of a thought able to embrace them all, be grounded in a will which, in producing them such as they are, accepts them such as they appear.[13]

God's very passivity, in the synthetic perception of multiple objects, is itself creative or, at least, constitutive.[14] God illu-

11. Virgoulay profitably refers readers to 459–61 of *L'Action* (1893); this corresponds to 418–21 of the English translation used here; see Maurice Blondel, *Action: Essay on a Critique of Life and a Science of Practice (1893),* trans. Oliva Blanchette (Notre Dame, Ind.: University of Notre Dame Press, 1984), 419. See Virgoulay, "Exégèse, théologie et philosophie," 568. See also van Hooff, "Panchristismus," 423ff, and Tilliette, "Philosophical Christology," 150. Van Hooff and Tilliette describe Blondel's notion of the interrelationship of activity and passivity as constitutive of meaning for man.

12. Antonelli summarizes nicely: "Blondel ha definito le condizioni trascendentali della perfetta consistenza della realtà: che questa eserciti una vera azione e che tale azione sia subita nella passione volontaria di un essere capace di una conoscenza assoluta della realtà stessa;" see Mario Antonelli, *L'Eucaristia nell' "Action" (1893) di Blondel: La chiave di volta di un'apologetica filosofica* (Milan: Glossa, 1991), 158.

13. Blondel, *Action (1893)*, 419.

14. Cf. Blondel, *Carnets intimes*, 1, 140: "Γνῶναι ἔστιν εἶναι τὸ μέτρον τοῦ ὄντως. C'est contenir le connu; c'est être devenu le contenu lui-même et en outre le dominer, étant l'unité contenante." Cf. Tilliette, "Le panchristisme dans L'Action," 48:

minates that which he sees, drawing the multiplicity of real things into intelligible unity; without this integration, things as such could not exist. There is no creation without solidification in God. No phenomenal-noumenal identity stands apart from things' creation by God and unifying reintegration into God by his embrace. In God's knowing the created thing, he makes the creature "be what is to be known, so that this known may have being."[15] Things then have an activity vis-à-vis God, yet only because God has freely allowed this in creation. Creation, to be real, must have an activity that is properly its own; it must impress, not simply receive, knowledge. Only God can, in receiving intelligibility, confer upon it an absolute and certain character.

Blondel circumvents the problems associated with attributing passivity to God by qualifying this thesis in a significant way. God does not enter as passive into a relationship with his creation as God *simpliciter*. Nor, at the other extreme, does he do this abstractly or by delegating this role to man, the summit of material creation.[16] Rather, this is accomplished in the mediating God-man.[17]

"[L]a consistance de l'ordre créé, l'enracinement dans l'être des choses sans pour-soi, supposent une conscience qui lie leur multiplicité et en même temps se soumet à leur présence."

15. Blondel, *Action (1893)*, 419.

16. Blondel, *Action (1893)*, 420. That, according to Blondel's logic, such a role could not be accomplished by man is indicated by Antonelli, *L'Eucaristia nell' "Action,"* 158–59 et passim.

17. See Sullivan, "Blondel, Christ and Creation," 66, 67. Virgoulay summarizes Blondel's understanding of the Word Incarnate as Mediator: "[I]l est comme la clef de voûte de l'univers, lui assurant cohérence et consistance ultime"; see Virgoulay, "Exégèse, théologie et philosophie," 568. Cf. van Hooff, "Panchristismus," 421: "Jesus Christus ist Grund, Synthese, Vermittler und Vollender der Wirklichkeit im ganzen"; 421–23 highlights the indispensably constitutive role of the Eucharistic

In *Action*, in a manner both transparent and veiled, reference to Christ intervenes to found and guarantee the reality and objectivity of the sensible world. Christ is the *Vinculum*, the universal lictor—it is he who binds together the multiple fasces of appearance, of phenomena. This is not some bewildering initiative; it is an aspect of the mystery hidden since the foundation of the world.[18]

Reality is grounded in the passive knowing of the Word Incarnate.[19] All human knowing rests on the knowing of Christ.[20]

---

Christ for reality (as will be seen below). See also Tilliette, "Maurice Blondel et la controverse christologique," 154–55. Cf. de Lubac, *Chardin, Blondel*, 38; writing to Auguste Valensin, Blondel says: "[I]n studying the conditions necessary for this "solidification" of the creature (a term borrowed from St. Augustine, *Confessions*, vol. XI, c. XXX), I found that the logical, metaphysical, moral, and religious avenues of my thought led to this ontogenetic and phylogenetic Pan-Christism which we have so often discussed together." See also Blondel, *Carnets intimes*, 1:113–14: "Le Médiator redouble la création: Tout a été fait par lui; mais rien encore ne serait sans lui; sans lui, tout ce qui a été fait serait néant, c'est-à-dire sans lui-même présent en son oeuvre, devenu son oeuvre, sans son regard, sans son humanité. On est ce qu'on connaît et ce qu'on aime. Rien ne peut être s'il n'est connu et aimé de Dieu; et par l'opération de l'homme, le Verbe est devenu monde, Verbum caro factum est.... L'union hypostatique est la consommation de la Création: l'Incarnation est comme une première Rédemption; la faute a rendu nécessaire à l'homme la grande Rédemption sanglante."

18. "Dans *L'Action*, d'une manière transparente et voilée, l'évocation du Christ intervient pour établir et garantir la réalité et l'objectivité du monde sensible. Le Christ est le *Vinculum*, le Licteur universel, il l'est aussi pour lier le multiple faisceau de l'apparence, du phénomène. Ce n'est pas une initiative déconcertante, c'est un aspect du mystère caché depuis la fondation du monde"; see Tilliette, "Maurice Blondel et la controverse christologique," 141.

19. "It would be the divine knowledge of the Mediator which guaranteed the stability, the permanence, the truth of what we know fleetingly, vaguely, inadequately, with little real grasp of its foundations, implications, interconnections or relationship with the whole" see Sullivan, "Blondel, Christ and Creation," 67. Sullivan refers to *L'Action*, 463–64 (Eng., 423). Here Blondel says, "Appearances themselves, duration, all the inconsistent forms of individual life, far from being abolished, participate in the absolute truth of the divine knowledge of the Mediator."

20. See Blondel and Valensin, *Correspondance*, 42–43; on 43 he says: "Nos connaissances ne sont *objectives* et l'objectif n'est *réel* que par l'Emmanuel, et si le Verbe est incarné." Tilliette, in "Philosophical Christology," 150, points to the constitutive role of this mediation for other human knowledge: "Gethsemani and Golgotha are

Jesus passively receives the activity of creatures, incorporating them in perception.[21] Writing to von Hügel, Blondel says:

> If we are for him, he is for us; he is literally the Son of Man. Moreover, if creation has its consistency in the perfect knowledge and loving will of Christ, then Christ has his singular reality through the universal consummation of all life and all being created in him. If (in one sense) he were not everything, he would be nothing and he would have nothing. I beseech you: recall our conversations ... my Panchristism, the Universal Constitutor [*Réalisateur*].[22]

---

the places par excellence where the consciousness of Christ gathers up consciousnesses and their lack of consciousness, while at the same time submitting to them and suffering them. The basis of intersubjective consciousness is compassion and charity, because the intersubjective bond is the consciousness of the dying Jesus."

21. The manner in which Blondel demurs from the unqualified statement that God perceives passively is further specified in the following lines, signaled to the present writer by an editorial mention in Blondel and Valensin, *Correspondance,* 46–47. An English translation is in Maurice Blondel, *The Letter on Apologetics and History and Dogma,* trans. Alexander Dru and Illtyd Trethowan (Grand Rapids, Mich.: William B. Eerdmans, 1964), 203: "Not, of course, that God is to be made passive, by reaction, to the activity of things or made subject to the necessity of perceiving or submitting to them in order really to produce them. But if we enter upon the labyrinth of sensible existence, if we consider that knowledge and being on this level form the first solid link in the whole chain of our representations and realize that the consistency and fixity of all the rest depends on it, and if finally we try to conceive the conditions on which all the realization of phenomena depends, including those which we call secondary or subjective qualities, those, in short, which manifestly presuppose, in order to exist, rational perception in a corporeal organism, then it will certainly seem that this reality must be inevitably conceived as bound up with the organic and rational activity of a mediator capable of attaching this form, inconsistent in itself, to the existence of the absolute being, who alone, in seeing, brings what he sees into existence, but who sees it aliter per divinitatem, aliter per carnem, whether one must find this mediating flesh in man united to the Word who enlightens every mind, and whose part would thus be to act as the universal bond of being throughout all history, or whether one must, in fact, have recourse to Christ's Incarnation itself." That which is implicit here ought to be emphasized, should one wish to entertain Blondel's idea of passively constituting knowledge. God is not passive before his creation; the Mediator passively perceives according to his human nature. Cf. Blondel, *Carnets intimes,* 1:53–54.

22. "[S]i nous sommes par Lui, il est par nous; qu'il est, à la lettre, le Fils de

In the vein of the creedal and Johannine affirmation that the Word is he "through whom all things were made," Blondel emphasizes the Incarnate state of the Word as the principle of creation.[23] As Incarnate the Word consummates the act of creation in knowing and loving it.[24] According to Blondel's often-quoted line, paraphrasing St. Bernard,[25] the Word stands within creation in concretizing and perfecting it: "That which he knew from eternity by his divinity, he learned otherwise in time by his experience in the flesh."[26] It is in this sense that Blondel says that Christ is best seen as immanent to creation, rather than simply as its summit.[27]

Down to the last detail of the last imperceptible phenomenon, mediating action makes up the truth and the being of all that is. And it

l'Homme; et que, si la Création a sa consistance en la connaissance parfaite et en la volonté amoureuse du Christ, le Christ a sa réalité singulière par l'universel aboutissement de toute vie et de tout être créé en lui. Si (en un sens) il n'était pas tout, il ne serait rien; et il n'y aurait rien. Souvenez-vous, je vous prie, de nos conversations ... sur mon Panchristisme, sur le Réalisateur universel"; see René Marlé, S.J., *Au coeur de la crise moderniste: Le dossier inédit d'une controverse* (Paris: Aubier, Éditions Montaigne, 1960), 136.

23. "Pour [Blondel] le Verbe incarné joue un rôle universel dans l'ordre de la création, depuis l'origine et pas seulement à partir de la vie terrestre de Jésus"; see Virgoulay, "Exégèse, théologie et philosophie," 569.

24. Cf. Blondel, *Carnets intimes*, 1:294. On Christmas Day, 1889, he wrote about Christ's nativity: "Dès lors la création est achevée; le monde a toute sa solidité." Cf. Tilliette, "Le panchristisme dans L'Action," 47: "[L]e monde a dans le Christ sa consistance, sa solidité, sa raison d'être." See also Emmanuel Gabellieri, "'Vinculum' et 'sursum': Métaphysique, christologie et ontologie trinitaire ou les 'exigences philosphiques du christianisme,'" in René Virgoulay, *Le Christ de Maurice Blondel* (Paris: Desclée, 2003), 190–91.

25. Van Hooff, "Panchristismus," 430, refers to De gradibus humilitatis et superbiae 3, 6, 10, and 23.

26. "Quod sciebat ab aeterno per divinitatem, aliter temporali didicit experimento per carnem"; see Blondel, *Action (1893)*, 420. Cf. Blondel, *Carnets intimes*, 1:280: "Le Christ, l'Homme est l'oeil de Dieu dans le monde."

27. See Marlé, *Crise moderniste*, 100 and 138.

would be strange indeed to be able to explain anything apart from Him without Whom nothing has been made, without Whom all that has been made falls back into nothingness.[28]

Little more than implicit in this exposition so far has been the idea that Christ's embracing of the human condition is part of God's plan from the beginning.[29] Blondel intends this not simply in the ordinary sense that God foreknows the Incarnation of his Son from eternity.[30] Rather, as we have seen above, creation depends on Incarnation. Inasmuch as God intended to create man in the way that he did, he also intended to become man. Christ is the beginning and end, the condition and purpose, of all creation.[31] This is, of course, to incline toward the position of Scotus in some form on the question of the conditioned or unconditioned predestination of the Incarnation.[32] It is also, however, to balance an understanding of the perfecting action of Christ in grace with a protological notion of Christ's foundation of the natural world.

28. Blondel, *Action (1893)*, 424. Cf. Blondel, *Carnets intimes*, 1:125: "Les choses créées et finies n'ont leur réalité pleine et originale que pour une sensibilité, pour l'Homme, créé et fini. Le Père a créé, mais le Verbe incarné a vu."

29. See Blondel, *Carnets intimes*, 1:108: "Il fallait que ce fût le Verbe, la Science de Dieu, qui vît par nos yeux et souffrît dans nos membres. Son incarnation fait la réalité de la création."

30. This, at least, is implied in 1 Pt 1:19–20.

31. "Est-ce votre humanité qui est la fin première et dernière de la Création? Sans doute: Primogenitus omnis creaturae"; see Blondel, *Carnets intimes*, 1:75.

32. There is no need to decide against Aquinas on the question of the predestination of the Incarnation in order to be faithful to Blondel's thought generally. Since God foreknew both the Fall and that his Son would become Incarnate to redeem man, one could say without contradiction that he also decided from eternity to involve the Incarnate Son in creation. Incarnation may remain conditioned by the Fall and the Incarnate Word may be the Mediator between creation and God if we realize with Blondel that God's plan is unitary in eternity. Much more would have to be said in elaboration and defense of this point, but here is not the place. See *ST* 3, 1, 3. Cf. Cointet, "Le Médiateur," 162 and 184.

Even from the natural perspective, human solidarity seems to have been constituted in view of the supernatural design that made Christ the single key of humanity and of the universe....

Addressing the thesis of Wehrlé, according to which human solidarity precedes and enables redemption, the natural being flatly prior to the supernatural, Blondel continues:

Your thesis has the liability of representing Christ as an artificial accessory, an *addition* after the fact, a bandage of last recourse.[33]

Since the Word is present as constitutively active in the world —since in him creation is established and stabilized—the world, in the actual order, is inconceivable apart from the engaged mediation of the Son. To this end, his destiny of Incarnation is of a piece with God's decision to create the world. Creation and the Redemption are two moments of the same design achieved by Christ.[34]

33. "[C]est ... que, même au point de vue naturel, la solidarité humaine semble avoir été constituée en vue du dessein surnaturel qui a fait du Christ le chef unique de l'humanité et de l'univers.... Dès lors votre thèse a l'inconvénient de nous montrer dans le Christ un accessoire postiche, un *ajout* après coup, un emplâtre pour l'usage externe"; see Marlé, *Crise moderniste,* 282 (my italics). Cf. de Lubac, *Chardin, Blondel,* 23: "One cannot remain true to Catholicism and be content with a mediocre explanation, a limited outlook which represents Christ as an accident of history, isolating Him in the Cosmos as if He were an episode without proper time and place. One cannot represent Him as an intruder, an alien in the crushing and hostile immensity of the universe." See also Blondel and Valensin, *Correspondance,* 44. Sullivan draws attention to the similarity between Blondel and Scotus regarding the motives for the Incarnation; see Sullivan, "Blondel, Christ and Creation," 64. Virgoulay correctly suggests that Blondel moves beyond Scotus. See also Virgoulay, "Exégèse, théologie et philosophie," 569; Virgoulay, "La christologie blondélienne," 72; Mouroux, "Conscience du Christ," 191; Theobald, "Christologie transcendentale," 443; Cointet, "Le Médiateur," 161 (esp. note 5) et passim; Gabellieri, "'Vinculum' et 'sursum,'" 199–200; Antonelli, *L'Eucaristia* nell' *"Action,"* 168; and Tilliette, "Maurice Blondel et la controverse christologique," 142.

34. That the Incarnate Word undertakes a passivity vis-à-vis sin in his suffering does not belong absolutely to God's design of creation but is an accounting for the

## LOVE AND SUFFERING

At the nadir of Blondel's descending Christological arc, we encounter an element that takes us back to the heart of his Panchristism. The depth of the Son's descent is suffering itself.

Created things are not simply known by the Incarnate Word. They are loved by the Son as constitutive of their being.

> The *Vinculum* is not just a physical nature, a metaphysical essence, an immanent finality: without prejudice to all of these, it is more the supreme magnet [*aimant*], which attracts and unites from above, level by level, the complete hierarchy of distinct and consolidated beings.[35]

To be is not only to be intelligible; it is also to be lovable and, more than that, to be loved concretely.

Two features of the love that unites all things are noteworthy. First, it is Crucified; second, it is concrete in the Eucharist. The latter issue will be discussed in the next section as the continuation of the former.

Christ embraces the human condition by means of a living incorporation of human experience down to its most inglorious features.[36] The created order rests on the Incarnation and

---

exercise of man's will. The Mediator embraces reality as it actually is and in its fallible freedom. See Antonelli, *L'Eucaristia nell' "Action,"* 166–68 and 191.

35. "[L]e *Vinculum* n'est pas seulement une nature physique, une essence métaphysique, une finalité immanente: il est encore, sans préjudice de tout cela, l'aimant suprême, qui attire et unit par en haut, étage par étage, la hiérarchie totale des êtres distincts et consolidés"; see Blondel and Valensin, *Correspondance*, 45. The words quoted are de Lubac's. (It is impossible to convey in translation the double meaning that is no doubt intended here: in addition to meaning magnet, "aimant" is the present participle of the verb to love, "aimer.")

36. See Blondel, *Carnets intimes*, 1:88–89. In lines redolent of Bonaventure, Blondel says: "Et Verbum caro factum est. Comment cela ? L'infini devient le fini,

any understanding of the cosmos as fallen necessarily passes through the Cross. The bestowal of absoluteness and stability on the perceived whole of creation and eo ipso on individuals extends from the divine Witness to creation in his corporeal experience of that creation; to redeem the world from its fallenness, he experiences it in its errant horror in the consummation of passivity and suffering that is the Crucifixion. Blondel says:

> Perhaps it was necessary that, having become flesh himself, [the Word] should become, through a passion at once necessary and voluntary, the reality of the determinism appearing in nature and the forced knowledge of objective phenomena, the reality of the voluntary failings and the privative knowledge which is their sanction, the reality of religious action and of the sublime destiny held in store for man fully consequent with his own willing. He it is who is the measure of all things.[37]

It is a comparatively straightforward matter to see, as we have above, that the Son could ground in knowing religious action, the reality of Heaven, and so on, but it is difficult to see how the Incarnate Word becomes the reality of sin and privative knowledge.[38]

Christ does not experience the lowliness of the human condition only in, for example, the meekness of sleeping his first hours in a manger but in confrontation with the ruin of sin and degradation. That which human persons suffer con-

---

la lumière est l'obscurité, l'esprit est le corps, l'être est le néant. Tout ce qui n'est pas en vous n'est pas. O lien substantiel, unité de vos créatures, vie de vos membres, être des êtres." See also Mouroux, "Conscience du Christ," 197–200. See Tilliette, "Le panchristisme dans L'Action," 53: "Rien d'humain ne lui est étranger. Il a pour ainsi dire épousé la vie de tous les hommes de tous les temps."

37. Blondel, *Action (1893)*, 420–21.

38. The question, of course, is not new. Cf. 2 Cor 5:21.

sciously and unconsciously in the fallen world become his with a piquancy intensified by that which he knows according to his divine Nature.

By being sensitive and suffering, Christ has acquired that which we ourselves acquire. At the same time, however, his divine knowledge has analogically enriched his imagination to the point that it has rendered him passive vis-à-vis the universe in a stigmatizing sympathy, conscious of our unconsciousness, of our sufferings, of our failures. He is truly man, because he is the man of all men; his humanity is guaranteed and, in a manner of speaking, constituted by ours. He is the Son of Man.[39]

Christ's theandric experience of sin's consequences, his becoming sin, fits the pattern of the mediating union of that which is experienced with the Absolute described above. In this connection, however, it must be borne in mind that that which is experienced is sin and that the Absolute is also Love itself.

39. "Le Christ a acquis, en être sensible et pâtissant, ce que nous acquérons nous-mêmes; mais en même temps sa science divine a enrichi analogiquement son imagination, su point que par une sympathie stigmatisante elle l'a rendu passif de l'Univers, conscient de nos inconsciences, de nos souffrances, de nos défaillances; il est vraiment homme, parce qu'il est l'homme de tous les hommes, son humanité est garantie et pour ainsi dire constituée par la nôtre, il est le Fils de l'homme"; see Marlé, *Crise moderniste*, 79. Cf. 135: "[L]a conscience de son humanité est faite de toutes nos consciences humaines." On Christ's being constituted by humanity and its experience, see Mouroux, "Conscience du Christ," 203–4. On 204 he says: "C'est pourquoi nous avons besoin du Christ pour subsister et nous achever, tandis que le Christ, en son humanité a besoin de nous pour être, humainement, le centre réel d'un univers réel; c'est pourquoi aussi la conscience du Christ est faite de toutes nos consciences (avec toutes leurs inconsciences), tandis que nos consciences ne trouvent leur lumière, leur salut, leur achèvement, que dans la conscience de Jésus-Christ." See 198: "Tout ce qui est un pâtir appartenant à la condition pécheresse, le Christ a voulu l'éprouver." See also Tilliette, "Maurice Blondel et la controverse christologique," 143, 149–53: "Il y a cette conscience humaine solidaire de toutes les consciences humaines." Cf. Virgoulay, "La christologie blondélienne," 65–67, 81–82.

## THE EUCHARIST

The Eucharist is the continuation of the Word Incarnate as the Vinculum substantiale.[40] Blondel writes:

> It is worth repeating: "the example of the Eucharist [is] not *one* application, one of many, of the *Vinculum*, but the perfect example, the definitive vehicle, the total and perfect realization of the Leibnizian hypothesis pushed toward the perspectives that it opens up before us....
>
> Transubstantiation, by substituting the natural being of bread and wine with the *Vinculum* of Christ himself, seems to be a prelude, under the veils of mystery, to the final assimilation, to the supreme incorporation in the Incarnate Word of all that exists: The Word was made flesh so that the flesh and all things may be assimilated to God through the Incarnation."[41]

40. Cf. Antonelli, *L'Eucaristia nell' "Action,"* which underscores this point effectively on, for example, 178: "È l'Eucaristia che opera la susistenza delle cose: *vinculum* che assicura la realtà oggettiva di tutto."

41. "(Il faut reprendre) 'l'exemple de l'Eucharistie non plus comme *une* application, *una e multis*, du *Vinculum*, mais comme l'exemplaire parfait, le véhicule décisif, la réalisation totale et parfaite de l'hypothèse leibnizienne poussée jusqu'au bout des perspectives qu'elle nous ouvre.... La Transsubstantiation, en substituant à l'être naturel du pain et du vin le Vinculum ipsius Christi, nous apparaît dès lors comme préludant sous les voiles du mystère à l'assimilation finale, à l'incorporation suprême de tout ce qui est au Verbe incarné: Verbum caro factum ut caro et omnia assimilarentur Deo per Incarnatum'"; see Blondel and Valensin, *Correspondance*, 45. The redacted form of this quotation belongs to de Lubac, who is quoting from *Une énigme historique, le "vinculum substantiale" d'après Leibniz et l'ébauche d'un réalisme supérieur*, the 1930 French version of Blondel's Latin thesis, 124. Cf. de Lubac, *Chardin, Blondel*, 23. Referring to this thesis on Leibniz's *Vinculum substantiale,* Blondel says, "This thesis deals with the problem of how matter 'achieves substance' by examining how the unity of the compound (which matter is) can attain corporeality; furthermore, the question raised by Leibniz and des Bosses concerning transubstantiation during the Eucharist leads us to conceive of Christ, without detriment to the constituent monads, as the bond which makes substantiation possible, the vivifying agent for all of creation: vinculum perfectionis."

If in the Incarnate Christ all things are integrated in loving knowledge, the Eucharist is the efficacious prolepsis of the final transformation or integration of all things into God. The leading edge of cosmic transformation is Eucharistic transubstantiation,[42] yet transformation and transubstantiation cannot be understood in the same way for Blondel. The idea of the reintegration of creation into God is not, for Blondel, a kind of eschatological pan(en)theism; rather, it indicates the intensified solidification and gratuitous perfection of creatures as creatures.

God's point of contact with man is the matter of the Eucharist.[43] Christ is active in the world as the Eucharist.[44] In the Eucharist, Christ assimilates the cosmos to himself. We will have in the following to apply the idea of assimilation in the Eucharist to the subject of sin.

## THE CHRIST OF SACRED HEART DEVOTION

Blondel's prephilosophical notion of Christ has been allowed to guide his philosophy.[45] On a more personal level,

42. Cf. Antonelli, *L'Eucaristia nell' "Action,"* 195.

43. Sullivan, "Blondel, Christ and Creation," 69. Cf. Antonelli, *L'Eucaristia nell' "Action,"* 170–71, 173–74, 181, et passim. Man's participation in God is also Eucharistic in the sense that in communion man has the possibility of participating in Christ's passive solidification of creatures. This is the condition on which life has meaning for man.

44. Van Hooff, "Panchristismus," 421: "Da diese alles verwirklichende Gegenwart Christi—eine gottmenschliche Gegenwart—'action' ist, kann ihr auch nur in einer 'action' entsprochen werden. Im Sakrament der Eucharistie wird die kosmische 'action' Christi begangen und gefeiert."

45. See Mouroux, "Conscience du Christ," 191, where Mouroux quotes Blondel's confession that the Incarnation, for him, guides everything. In English: "[P]erhaps prior to all other philosophical questions … the problem of the Incarnation seemed to me to be the touchstone of a true cosmology, a metaphysics

his thought has been informed by his devotional life.[46] This is true specifically of his devotion to the Sacred Heart.[47] Jean Mouroux, in his masterful treatment of Blondel's Christology, indicates that the latter's totalizing, prephilosophical option for Christianity is rooted in his personal dedication to this devotion.[48] Sacred Heart devotion, with which many Christians are already very familiar, involves a notion of Christ who, even in his glory, is wounded by the sin and indifference of humanity and continues to condescend to being consoled by believers in his pain.[49] Apparently in some tension with this, Blondel defines a high, transcendent Christology over against the Modernist trajectory of Alfred Loisy. For example, the Christ of the Panchristism described above, who unites perception of creation to the Absolute, also knows that he is God at all times.[50] At once we see the need of reconciling the low

complete within itself"; see de Lubac, *Chardin, Blondel*, 23. The French can be found in Blondel and Valensin, *Correspondance*, 47. On Blondel's Christian influence as the driving force of his philosophy, see van Hooff, "Panchristismus," 416–18 and 421–22.

46. "Blondel était de longue date pratiquant … d'une voie royale : l'accès mystique et spirituel de l'âme à la personne de Jésus de Nazareth.… [S]i la psychologie du Christ importait tant à Blondel, c'est qu'elle était pour lui une affaire actuelle et que le contact ne devait pas être coupé du Christ vivant accessible à sa prière au Christ prêchant et souffrant connu par les Evangiles. Le Christ ne saurait être divisé"; see Tilliette, "Maurice Blondel et la controverse christologique," 145. For a detailed treatment of Blondel's devotional life and its role in his thought, see Yvette Périco, "De la foi au Christ à la Christologie philosophique," in *Le Christ de Maurice Blondel*, ed. René Virgoulay (Paris: Desclée, 2003), 11–34.

47. See, e.g., Blondel, *Carnets intimes*, 1:89: "Ah! formez mon pauvre coeur à l'image du vôtre, si vaillant, si dévoué, si humble."

48. Mouroux, "Conscience du Christ," 187; cf. 198.

49. Cf. Blondel, *Carnets intimes*, 1:511: "Daignez demain me ressusciter, me changer, m'améliorer. Que beaucoup d'âmes soient prêtes: la belle soirée que ce devrait être! la terre devrait valoir davantage en ce moment; et votre coeur être consolé."

50. More than one author offers a helpful description of this controversy; one

Christology of Sacred Heart devotion with the high Christology of Blondel's Panchristism.

The idea of the Sacred Heart is raised at this point with twofold purpose. In the first place we are puzzled by the issue just mentioned: How could Blondel have been personally involved with a devotion that seems to be at variance with his publicly maintained transcendent Christology? Is not the tension here heightened by the fact that his thought owes something to his devotion, that he practiced a kind of philosophy on one's knees? This question would remain one of a merely idle and historical curiosity were it not for the fact that it affords at least the hope of satisfying a deeper problem. Without following Blondel in every particular of his Christological vision, I proffer the suggestions, in no way novel, firstly that a protological Christology—highlighted today, for example, by Luis Ladaria—one in short that applies a maximalist interpretation to Col 1:15ff—ought to be taken seriously and secondly that such a Christology in no way implies the docetism that Blondel sought to avoid. Christ is the firstborn[51] precisely of that creation that groans and suffers together.[52] The idea of the Sacred Heart, then, appears as a sort of test case or as a field on which to further an understanding of redemption and suffering that is compatible with Blondel's Christology.

Blondel's Christ is not totalizing and transcendent in spite of human burden but precisely because of it; Sacred Heart de-

example from Blondel's correspondence with Loisy will suffice: "[N]ier la conscience divine de Jésus, c'est nier la divinité du Christ"; see Marlé, S.J., *Crise moderniste*, 78.

51. Col 1:15.

52. Rm 8:22.

votion, as we will see, does not suggest a Christ who is engulfed by suffering but the Redeemer who has circumscribed it.[53]

## SYNTHESIS?

Christ's sufferings, for Blondel,[54] are entailed by his decision to experience all that his sinful creation experiences. He seems to have meditated on the relation of these sufferings to redemption[55] and, as mentioned, sought to console Christ in the suffering of his Heart. But at this point a serious question presents itself or, better said, has been pulling at us all along. What can it mean to say, with the Paray-le-Monial form of the devotion, that our sins still injure Christ's Sacred Heart and that Christ grieves even now over our indifference to his love?[56] Perhaps it is not a stretch to think that Blondel took these words seriously.[57] No doubt Blondel is speaking somewhat poetically when

53. Cf. Tilliette, "Maurice Blondel et la controverse christologique," 156–57: "Maurice Blondel, lui, avait opté résolument avec toute la tradition pour la christologie dite descendante. Mais son sens de l'Incarnation, de la Condescendance, est tel que la charité excessive du Verbe divin ne s'arrête qu'au Fils de l'Homme, à l'Homme de tous les hommes, mieux, à l'Homme des douleurs."

54. Since Blondel's Christology is not developed, specific questions, such as the ones addressed at this point, can at only be approached from perspectives that seem to fit within his broad vision. I have attempted, where possible, to indicate a resonance between specific considerations and the Christology adumbrated above. That which follows is an attempt to provide a Christological complement to Blondel's thought, yet herein something other than the strictly Blondelian will undoubtedly be found.

55. "Sans doute, les opprobres et les tortures ont été sensibles à votre chair et à votre coeur, et pourtant vous les acceptiez avec une fervente impatience, tant l'amour vous pressait"; see Blondel, *Carnets intimes*, 1:107.

56. See, e.g., Jean V. Bainvel, S.J., *Devotion to the Sacred Heart: The Doctrine and Its History*, 7th ed., trans. E. Leahy (London: Burns, Oates and Washbourne, 1924), 20–21. As a side note, Bainvel was a cautious admirer of Blondel's thought; see Blondel and Valensin, *Correspondance*, 1:89–90.

57. See Blondel, *Carnets intimes*, vol. 2 (1894–1949) (Paris: Les Éditions du

he says that there are evils "that make God suffer,"[58] yet he cannot be dismissed. However it may be, Pius XII is equally clear about the Sacred Heart in Haurietis aquas, 85: "That Heart indeed is no longer subject to the emotional disturbances of our mortal condition."[59] Are we at an impasse? It would seem that we are required to choose at this point between mysticism and Magisterium. Have we not also descended to a very particular point here while having lost sight of the larger question of this chapter? It should become clear that a solution to the particular issue at hand, the verbal discrepancy between Sr. Margaret Mary's revelation and Pope Pius XII, is at the same time the beginning of an insight into our larger question.

In response it is certainly tempting to pit private against public revelation or poetry against doctrine. We could argue that Sr. Margaret Mary's purported experiences are trumped by Pius XII's indication that Christ does not suffer because, though per se the encyclical in which this statement is found does not carry the note of infallibility, it witnesses to the continual teaching of the Church and certainly belongs to its ordinary teaching authority. The Church in canonizing Sr. Margaret Mary did not directly condone her claims, after all.

We could also take refuge in a distinction between poetic theological discourse and doctrine sensu stricto. Margaret Mary's vision would belong to poetry or metaphor, akin to

Cerf, 1966), 109: "[J]e veux que ma plus grande peine, que ma seule peine soit celle que vous éprouvez en face de l'état du monde, en face de mon défaut de générosité chrétienne." Noteworthy is the present sense of Christ's suffering.

58. In his words: "qui font souffrir Dieu . . ."; Blondel, *Carnets intimes*, 1:294.

59. Translation from *Heart of the Saviour*, ed. Josef Stierli (Freiburg: Herder & Herder, 1957). See Jeanne Weber, O.S.B., "Devotion to the Sacred Heart: History, Theology and Liturgical Celebration," *Worship* 72, no. 3 (1998): 236–54, 249.

biblical statements that God is a fortress, while the Pius XII would be taken to speak unequivocally.

Though each of these solutions has something to recommend it, we must be on guard against trivializing the insights of a mystic. The saints, as von Balthasar reminds us, mean what they say. Yet no saint, or theologian for that matter, means what he or she says just as he or she says it; rather, Christian hope rests on the need and ability to liberate that which we say about God and the glorified God-man from imperfections that properly belong to as-yet-unglorified creatures. Eye has not seen and ear has not heard, but we should not for that cease speaking; we hope in that which we do not see but which we suggest with language. The "just enough" that we can say is our ground for hope; yet standing on this ground we cannot reach the zenith of God's own meaning in himself or in his dealings with us. The present case is no exception. The paradoxically true-but-not-adequate form must be distinguished from the limitations inherent in our conceptual clay. That Christ is wounded by our sin even today is not a meaningless phrase, but it is not for that true in the way that we say it. If we choose to repeat that Christ suffers our sin (in his glory, not simply during his lifetime), we seem to mean, plainly enough, that he experiences a physical or psychological alteration for the worse because of our misdeeds and that he remains injured and passive before them. Our specific notions of passivity and suffering, however, are the elements that must be purged from thought.[60] It will be asked

60. This is not to say that there is not an undergoing in Christ (according to his human nature) that is not in violence to human nature, for example, that of the passive intellect, which remains in the glorified state as it belonged to the preternatural Adam. See *ST* 1, 97, 2.

whether there ever was anything else to our idea. What remains after the suffering is removed from suffering?

Suffering entails what we may describe, with unavoidable metaphor, as a taking-in. In the glorious suffering of Christ described by Paray-le-Monial devotion we must retain the sense of Christ's Heart taking sin in, in the way that every heart takes blood in, in order to allow it to issue from this Heart with a different, inverted, meaning. Christ's power—which is not exhausted or consummated at one historical moment except if one understands that consummation to be a beginning with respect to both past and future[61]—is to stand evil on its head, to make of it a divine joke. No greater evil can be imagined, if Anselm is correct, than the murder of the God-man; the good that comes through this murder simply cannot be imagined.[62] The greatest evil is the source for the greatest good, yet there is not an organic connection between these two. Rather, the good from sin is not any the more due to sin than is the Incarnation.[63] Christ's love does violence to sin in bending its force against its intended course.[64] The negative value of sin becomes the positive value of goodness and redemption not, again, by anything intrinsic to sin but by what Christ does with sin as his unwilling instrument. This is nothing else but that which the tradition has meant by the saying

61. Cf. Maurice Blondel, *La Psychologie dramatique du mystère de la passion a Oberammergau* (Paris: Librairie Bloud & Cie, 1910), 45: "[L]a mort ne termine rien: elle est plutôt un commencement. Le Drame du Calvaire n'est jamais achevé, puisqu'il se perpétue en nous et pour nous."

62. 1 Cor 2:9.

63. See *ST* 3, 1, 3.

64. Cf. Blondel, *Carnets intimes*, 1:355: "[V]ous eussiez été déshonoré et amoindri; vous avez voulu épuiser; l'ignominie, l'outrage, la torture.... O mépris des apparences et force de l'amour qui transfigure toutes choses et intervertit tous les rôles!"

that God does not permit an evil except where he knows he can bring a greater good therefrom.[65] In his suffering he has taken up all of human sin and suffering[66] but not that suffering may be allowed its own dynamism.

"The heart takes into account,"[67] as Paul Claudel has it; the divine Heart of Jesus takes sin in to define thereby its parameters, that it may be "quantified," if negatively, and overcome. The God who works, as a familiar interpretation of the divine name in Ex 3:14 runs, continues to work in ongoing human history and it is indispensable to bear in mind that his mode of working is not substantially different post-Resurrection than it is during the Passion; indeed it could not be.

The heart is the symbolic (in the truest sense) locus of personal concentration.[68] Since concrete personal meaning is achieved in virtue of relations (to nature, animals, and, most significantly, to other persons) and these relations are marked by experiences, personal reality must in some way enfold the experiences that have been undergone. Essential in this, and

65. See *ST* 1, 2, 3, ad 1m, wherein Thomas cites Augustine, *Enchiridion* 11. Cf. Blondel, *Carnets intimes*, 1:201: "[D]'un plus grand mal vous tirez souvent un plus grand bien par un plus grand pardon. J'implore de vous cette transsubstantiation morale."

66. Blondel, *Carnets intimes*, 1:540: "Vous avez pris en vous et connu par votre amour tout ce que les hommes ont souffert et surtout tout ce dont ils ont eu tort de ne pas souffrir."

67. "[L]e coeur prend compte"; see Paul Claudel, "Le Coeur compte," in *Le Coeur*, ed. Paul Claudel (Bruges: Desclée de Brouwer, 1950), 12.

68. Karl Rahner, S.J., "'Behold This Heart!': Preliminaries to a Theology of Devotion to the Sacred Heart," in *Theological Investigations,* vol. 3, ed. Karl Rahner, S.J., trans. Karl-Heinz and Boniface Kruger (Baltimore and London: Helicon Press and Darton, Longman & Todd, 1967), 323, and Karl Rahner, S.J., "Some Theses for a Theology of Devotion to the Sacred Heart," in *Theological Investigations,* vol. 3, ed. Karl Rahner, S.J., trans. Karl-Heinz and Boniface Kruger (Baltimore and London: Helicon Press and Darton, Longman & Todd, 1967), 324, 336, and 344.

to the point of a modern misunderstanding about experience, is that while experience may be incorporated immediately and palpably, it is not experience itself that gives meaning but the relations that experience heralds, introduces, and seals.

The man that is himself a microcosm[69] defines himself, albeit not essentially but concretely, by means of relations on a microcosmic scale. Christ, as we have seen, accomplishes the same on a macrocosmic scale. Perhaps it is in this sense that Blondel maintains that the Word did not take on *a* human nature, but *the* human nature.[70] If the heart is, as Rahner suggests, that from which we give ourselves away in order to find ourselves in the reciprocity of these relations,[71] then it must not be surprising that Christ becomes, in the same rhythm of alienation and integration, the Heart of the world.

All of these themes, stated baldly, may seem to be so many truisms. Yet, taken together, we cannot mistake the course that they lead us along and an answer to our question comes more clearly into view. It is because Christ is the Heart of the world, this fact resting as it does on his having taken in his world in its sin, that the sinful world is redeemed. This is our foundation for understanding how Christ continues to suffer our sin. He still takes our sin in, as his Heart took in the wounding lance, in order to cover the lance with the blood that blanches garments[72] and the water that purifies souls.[73] Christ continues the same

69. Bonaventure, Itinerarium mentis in Deum, 2.

70. See Marlé, *Crise moderniste*, 240, as indicated by, among others, Mouroux, "Conscience du Christ," 203.

71. Rahner, "Behold This Heart!" 324.

72. Rev 7:14.

73. Cf. Blondel, *Carnets intimes*, 1:290: "Ne permettez pas que j'erre trop

taking-in of sin as the Church's eternal High Priest in order to return sin to us, denatured and captive as grace unto glory.

The suffering taking-in of Christ on Calvary is linked to a glorious taking-in of Christ in redemption—one does not function without the other. Glory is unthinkable without the Cross in the current economy of salvation. Had Christ not triumphed over suffering, were he not to continue his triumph over suffering (it should not need to be specified, without actually suffering now), the victory would be at best incomplete and the return only partial. The having-suffered is constitutive of his glory; his glory confers meaning on his having-suffered. Christ's taking-in continues, but its mode is necessarily changed. The victory that swallows up the death that is sin must be taken as no less real than the "offensive" character of sin and the suffering of Christ on earth.

Sin, or its consequence, remains the having-been-suffered but only, after Christ's glorification, as *aufgehoben* by or as sublated to victory. Moreover, we can see the same logic of movement, not only between victory and sins of the historical past, but between victory and sins of the present as well. That which one does today to "offend" God is or has already been seized and denatured by the Passion-into-Resurrection.[74] In a very real sense, then, Christ could tell a person of St. Margaret Mary's time or of ours that his or her sins and indifference

longtemps dans ce désert aride de la pensée, sans rencontrer la source qui jaillit du rocher, sans rencontrer votre présence même, au puits de Jacob, dans cette Samarie qu'il me faut visiter sans rencontrer, ô bon Jésus, la plaie désaltérante de votre coeur. Vous vous êtes épuisé pour nous emplir."

74. Cf. Blondel, *Carnets intimes*, 1:144: "Dieu transforme et divinise la partie irrationnelle et révoltée de notre être."

are injurious to himself. Christ ever is having-been-offended by sin. Redemption rests inexorably on that fact. This is the Catholic preference for the Crucifix to the unladen Cross.

Even a cursory and partial look at Christ's triumph over sin cannot end here. An account of Christ's suffering in the world and glory through and beyond the world must take into consideration the ongoing suffering of his people on earth. Indeed it is through this consideration, and not in attempting to account for it as an afterthought, that we come to a fuller understanding of everything that has been said so far. Augustine's meditation on Paul's notion of the ecclesial body of Christ, including in its suffering aspect,[75] affords him a profound insight into the exchange of suffering between members and the Head. Referring to Christ's agony in the Garden in connection with Ps 86, Augustine writes:

> He prolonged his prayer throughout the night, the gospel tells us, and at a later time, as he continued in prayer, drops of blood ran down his body. What did that suggest, when drops of blood oozed from his body as he prayed? Surely that the Church, which is his body, was already dripping with the blood of its martyrs.[76]

Christ suffers in his Church in some way.[77] This does not mean that Christ only suffers generally in the globality that

75. Cf. Col 1:24.

76. St. Augustine, "Exposition of Psalm 85," in *The Works of St. Augustine: A Translation for the 21st Century,* vol. 18, ed. John E. Rotelle, O.S.A., trans. Maria Boulding, O.S.B. (New York: New City Press, 2002), 221. Cf. Acts 9:4, 22:7, and 26:14. Many have noted the first-person use here: "Saul, Saul, why are you persecuting *me*?"

77. Cf. Tilliette, "Maurice Blondel et la controverse christologique," 147: "La durée de l'Eglise—'Jésus-Christ continué'—et le développement du dogme font aussi partie du panchristisme."

is his corporate extension. Rather we must be more specific. Christ suffers in each member of his mystical body, in each person whose emotions and experiences he has already suffered.[78] Only in insisting on the grammatically perfect sense of Christ's suffering—that he does not unequivocally suffer now but that he has suffered—can we meaningfully say that the suffering of each person incorporated into Christ's body is part of Christ's glory. We cannot in this new, ecclesial consideration lose sight of the fact that, as suffering has been and is transformed in Christ, the note of this transformation is also historically and concretely present in human suffering today in germinal form and as proleptic of the final consummation of history and cosmic transformation in Christ.[79] One's sufferings are not simply the glory of Christ but one's own glory in Christ even now. Suffering in Christ's Sacred Heart gives one's own suffering new meaning.[80] The efficacious archetype of this transformation is the Eucharist.[81] Physical bodies—those of bread and of believers—become, in different ways, his body. This mystery is predicated on the reality that our suffer-

78. Cf. Blondel, *La passion a Oberammergau*, 23: "[L]a Passion divine est, par définition, tellement universelle qu'elle pénètre réellement chacun de nous et que le drame est tout entier au coeur de tous."

79. Perhaps the line repeated most often in Blondel's diary is Ecce nova facio omnia. Cf. Blondel, *Carnets intimes*, 1:187: "La vraie fontaine de Jouvence, c'est la douleur, la Passion." Cf. Blondel, *Carnets intimes*, 1:244–45, where Blondel writes about "les douleurs . . . transformées en éternité."

80. Cf. Blondel, *Carnets intimes*, 1:414: "Du coeur de Marie au coeur de Jésus. Par le progrès de la dévotion littérale, vous savez raviver les ardeurs intimes de l'âme et donner sous le symbole un mystérieux aliment à l'amour insatiable. Votre coeur ne nous a été montré et livré que percé. Il n'y aura point de jour où pour vous je ne doive sentir, accepter, désirer ce coupe de lance: il nous est proposé de tant de côtes!"

81. Cf. Cointet, "Le Médiateur," 178.

ings have been taken up into the glory that is his and, on that condition, ours.[82]

Have we gone too far in "demythologizing" devotion to the Sacred Heart? There is no reason to deny that those words which Margaret Mary Alacoque reported are true, only it must be said that the sand exists now only as the pearl.

Sacred Heart devotion does not imply a Christ who suffers now in the plain sense of that phrase; Christ's *kenosis* in the immanent experience of suffering does not threaten his transcendence: Blondel's lived theological vision does not suffer from an internal inconsistency. As Christ's human experience is joined to the Absolute as the constituting condition of creation, so the sin that Christ has experienced is ever joined to his absolute Love. The elements that seemed to be in contradiction instead bear each other as conditions, for kenotic suffering is the transubstantiated matter of Christ's totalizing victory.[83]

82. Cf. Blondel, *Carnets intimes*, 1:317–18: "Et comme un peu de pain devient, par une parole, le Christ vivant, que tous nos actes, par une intention droite et haute, construisent le corps mystique de Dieu. C'est par eux que le monde entier doit être transsubstantié: ce miracle ne s'accomplit directement que dans le seul mystère de l'Eucharistie, pour nous apprendre à transfigurer aussi, à surnaturaliser le plus humble grain de blé, la plus infime de nos occupations." Elsewhere, in this connection, Blondel refers to "nos âmes surnaturellement transsubstantiées par l'adoption divine"; see Blondel, *Carnets intimes*, 2:271. Cf. Périco, "La foi au Christ," 20–21: "La nature humaine … a besoin d'une transformation.… L'eucharistie est encore le moyen de cette nécessaire métamorphose, moyen à chaque communion, moyen en de multiples recommencements, moyen d'une lente divinisation." Cf. Antonelli, *L'Eucaristia nell' "Action,"* 119: "[N]ella comunione la tentazione prometeica di essere Dio si muta in realtà 'graziosa.'"

83. Cf. Virgoulay, "Postface," 206: "Le Christ de Blondel est avant tout le Christ glorieux.… S'il insiste sur la kénose, c'est qu'il présuppose la gloire."

[ 3 ]

# CHARITY IN CHRIST AND TRUE INFINITY

The effect of Hegel's philosophy on theology, either in the elaboration of theological statements or in the wholesale rejection of the theological endeavor, can scarcely be overestimated. As the Hegelian dialectic was the driving force behind Feuerbach's and Marx's denials of God, so has Hegel's thought inspired twentieth-century theologians as different as Karl Rahner and Wolfhart Pannenberg. While some theological effort has been made toward an appropriation of the Hegelian understanding of the infinite in articulating the idea of God, the relation of Hegel's infinity to Christology and the virtues that unite persons to God is undeveloped. In this chapter I suggest that Hegel's notion of true infinity serves analogously to illuminate the Christian understanding of virtue, especially the virtue of charity. Following on this, I suggest that such a notion of virtue begins to round out and complete the perspectives on the salvific mediatorship of Jesus Christ offered in the first two chapters of this book. Christ's role as Mediator is really impossible if he does not bring the finite and fallen into the embrace of the infinite holiness of God. Since the finite is also free, this presupposes not simply a representative voluntary action on Christ's part but rather a voluntary movement that generates and sustains other free actions of the same kind. Thus, one of the implications of the union of the infinite and the finite in that of God and man is that the virtues that Christ freely and capitally embodied are both concretized and rooted in his own Person such that, in the current economy of salvation, there is no practice of virtue that is not *in* Christ himself.[1]

## ABSOLUTE VIRTUE

### *True Infinity*

I mean neither to draw out nor to rely on all possible implications of Hegel's understanding of infinity. Hegel's indication that a problem lies embedded in the common conception of infinity is more insightful and relevant to the present argument than is his elaboration of a solution to this problem. I will begin by maintaining that his understanding of "bad infinity" (*das Schlect-Unendliche*) helps us to bring to the fore a fuller meaning of love and the other virtues, which is implicit in their traditional, even Thomistic, descriptions.

1. Of course, the idea that virtue is practiced *after* or on the model of Christ belongs to the historical foundations of Christianity. St. Thomas reflects this ancient understanding in *Summa contra gentiles* 4, 54, art. 7 and *ST* 3, 1, 2.

As is well known, Hegel suggested that the common conception of infinity is merely privative: the in-finite is understood simply as the not-finite. The mind has recourse to one notion, the finite, over against which it proceeds to define the infinite. In this a paradox is already evident: the infinite cannot be so de*fin*ed for that is to limit the infinite to that against which it stands in relief. An infinite that is bordered by that which it is not cannot be truly infinite (*wahrhaft Unendliches*). Hegel's insight here is redolent of classical metaphysics in its insistence that God is not a being alongside other beings, which is implicit, for example, in the idea that God works through secondary causes. Yet Hegel brings into particular clarity the difficulty inherent in expressing any idea of infinity. Once infinity has become a particular thought—or is a thought "unthought" in reference to its opposite—infinity itself has already slipped away. Infinity is not limitless if *what* it is is precisely *that which it is not:* the finite. Again, the particular solution that Hegel's *Logic* puts before us in working toward a notion of infinity purified from limitation need not trouble us here.[2] It does belong to the scope of the present discussion, however, to indicate the way in which "bad infinity" ought to serve as a kind of negative clue in elucidating an understanding of true virtue.

2. See Hegel's *Science of Logic,* I, 2, C, in Stephen Houlgate, *The Opening of Hegel's Logic: From Being to Infinity,* Purdue University Press Series in the History of Philosophy (West Lafayette, Ind.: Purdue University Press, 2006). Wolfhart Pannenberg's adaptation of Hegel's argument, alluded to above, has also served as a helpful explanation. Cf. the illuminating explanation of infinity of McTaggart, who, in a certain respect, prefers Hegel's presentation of this subject in the *Encyclopedia* to that in the *Logic;* see John McTaggart Ellis McTaggart, *A Commentary on Hegel's Logic* (New York: Russell & Russell, 1964), 30–35.

### *Infinity and Virtue*

We are often tempted in practice to define virtue with respect to that which it is not, that is, to provide a principally negative definition of virtue. Virtue is taken as limited to the concrete and finite conditions of its exercise, to proscriptions and prescriptions, and even conceptually to the nonbeing that is evil. Under this aspect, virtue often remains self-enclosed and denied that movement beyond itself in which is found its true meaning. The moral norm that underpins virtue loses its center as the safeguard of a personal relationship and instead falls into the mold of the "law" of Paul or the "duty" that, for a time, obsessed the postcritical Western world. In redress, the Hegelian understanding of infinity functions as a useful analogy for understanding virtue correctly. When virtue is misconstrued as habitual legalism or submission to a capricious despotism, the moral agent fails to transcend the finite. Morality is not liberating here; rather, the norm that the moral agent has finitized into law serves as a fence or limitation rather than as an openness to infinity.

Value ethicists rightly teach that norms protect values, while recent ordinary papal teaching and other voices have emphasized that they safeguard relationships. Properly understood, the moral norm is transparent. It refers beyond itself to the Absolute Thou of a personal relationship. It respects the value of the Thou and protects that of the human person in relation to the Thou. In this way, the human person is guarded in the very depths of his or her meaning by the moral norm since, in reflection of the character of Trinitarian Persons, his or her personhood *is* his or her relationship.[3] Since a real, constitutive relationship connects the moral agent to God, this agent is not authentically himself or herself where and to the degree that he or she fails this relationship. We will see then that morality is revelatory of the person because it specifies the conditions on which human identity emerges in the light of the Thou.

As we will discuss shortly, Christ has colored and transformed the relationship between God and the human person with supernatural charity. Since this is the case, neither the human-divine relationship nor the human person constituted by this relationship are finally subject to that person's own control and determination. An obligation in justice to observe the boundaries specified by the Creator already binds human persons. In the current existential in which human persons have a supernatural vocation, however, they are doubly bound to observe God's norms and doubly indigent of the wherewithal to do so; sin would put even a purely natural finality out of reach. A fortiori, the norms that pertain specifically to the person's supernatural vocation are difficult to understand and fulfill. These standards, since they do not come from the human person, can appear as excessive rather than as exceeding. Were it not for the fact that grace here superabounds, the outcome would be a heteronomous appropriation of morality, in which the person sees the imperative of virtue in the all-too-human terms of competing wills. In such a reception of divine law, the

3. Fritz Wilhelmsen rightly cautions against exaggerating such a claim; the human person's meaning is not strictly and simply *Esse ad*; see Frederick D. Wilhelmsen, *The Metaphysics of Love* (New York: Sheed & Ward, 1962), 39–40.

person himself or herself is hemmed in, like the heteronomously conceived will he or she adopts or rejects, by the finite. Yet—and this is the grain of truth in Feuerbach's use of the Hegelian dialectic—the experience of heteronomy is one through which the person must often pass in order to come to terms with his or her relation to infinity. The Old Man is smashed on the rocks of the law in order for one to find oneself the New Man, in fidelity to the Thou's call.[4] In this new condition moral actions are done "willingly, readily, and delightfully."[5]

The moral agent must come to identify with the author and guarantor of morality, then, in order to live morality as interpersonal. This identification is also important on another level. Relation to the Thou is also the principle of the mature

4. Cf. Henri de Lubac, S.J., "A Meditation on the Principle of the Moral Life," *Communio* 26 (1999): 418–28, 419–20, including note 3: "Now, in proportion as this obligation [to tend toward a supernatural vocation] molds man, it tends to reveal its hidden essence. In proportion as it unveils its ideal, it loses the mask it had to wear for the sake of the initial training of the human animal—the mask of a harsh external constraint, of a positive code commanding or forbidding certain particular actions, of a law threatening with arbitrary sanctions. In being interiorized, it becomes all the more demanding. But the obedience that it requires increasingly takes the form of an assent.... To the same extent it therefore ushers in a higher freedom—and will do so in proportion as the precepts of the positive law increasingly become means. At the extreme, in the state of perfect freedom brought about by perfect obedience, obligation disappears, since it was never anything but a liberating constraint for the sake of this state of freedom." For de Lubac, the assent that follows obedience comes to disclose itself as from the attraction of the Supreme Good and, ultimately, that of Supreme Love.

5. "[V]oluntarie et prompte et delectabiliter"; St. Thomas Aquinas, *De caritate,* 2. Thomas's inspiration is Aristotle. For the Stagirite, the possession of a virtue is marked by pleasure in its exercise or, at least, the absence of pain. See, e.g., the *Nicomachean Ethics*, 4, 13–14, where Aristotle characterizes the act of right giving: καὶ ταῦτα ἡδέως ἢ ἀλύπως τὸ γὰρ κατ᾽ ἀρετὴν ἡδὺ ἢ ἄλυπον, ἥκιστα δὲ λυπερόν; see Aristotle, *Nicomachean Ethics,* trans. H. Rackham, Loeb Classic Library, Aristotle, XIX, 73 (Cambridge, Mass., and London: Harvard University Press and William Heinemann, 1934), 192–93.

self-distinction of the I.[6] Since it serves to protect and specify the relationship between I and Thou in a fundamental way, the moral norm facilitates the emergence of selfhood. Paradoxically, even as the Thou serves as a key principle of identification for the I, it draws the I out of and away from itself. In fidelity to itself, the I's intentionality remains in the other of its origin; it stands only to lose itself in fixating on itself.[7] In this we see clearly that the relationship between the two interlocutors, one human and the other divine, cannot be a relationship of simple opposition. The heteronomous observance of law, although noble in some sense and even the occasion of heroic self-sacrifice, conceals that identification with the Thou which is the condition for the finite self's realization in the supernatural tincture of infinity. Where the I emerges over against a misunderstood Thou, in mere opposition, its stature is invariably compromised. The person comes to full stature in the context of infinity. True moral action places the person here not as alien but in intimacy.

Moral virtue carries within itself an openness to infinity, but by this fact it also involves the risk that this openness, like

6. Martin Buber, *I and Thou,* 2nd ed., trans. Ronald Gregor Smith (New York: Charles Scribner's Sons, 1958), 24–29. Cf. von Balthasar's nod to Buber in a strikingly similar passage in Hans Urs von Balthasar, *Love Alone: The Way of Revelation* (London: Sheed & Ward, 1968), 61–62.

7. "The single presupposition of a genuine state of prayer is . . . the readiness of the whole man for [God's] Presence, simple turned-towardness, unreserved spontaneity. This spontaneity, ascending from the roots, succeeds time and again in overcoming all that disturbs and diverts. But in this our stage of subjectivized reflection not only the concentration of the one who prays, but also his spontaneity is assailed. The assailant is consciousness, the over-consciousness of this man here that he is praying, that he is *praying*, that *he* is praying"; see Martin Buber, *Eclipse of God: Studies in the Relation between Religion and Philosophy,* trans. Norbert Guterman, Maurice Friedman, Eugene Kamenka, and I. M. Lask (New York: Harper & Row, 1957), 126.

infinity itself, will be conceptually bound to the finite and compromised in its relational power. Virtue is truly absolute, in the etymological sense of this term: it is unbound, "freed from" limitation. It remains for us to specify this idea in its relation to love and Christ's redemption, but one final comment about moral virtue's transcendence of the finite must find a place in our discussion first. The absolute character of virtue and its norm does not lead in the direction of antinomianism. So far, I have used the term "law" in a restricted, somewhat pejorative sense, but it goes without saying that the term can mean much more. Law (in the broad sense) is instrumental in its own eventual sublation into love. "*Dilige et quod vis fac*" (Love and do what you want) is unclear until love's defense in rules is explicitly known; only then can love's authentic application be connatural.[8] Counterintuitively in this case, instinct follows pedagogy. The law comes to be written on one's heart; it is sublated, not discarded.[9]

## *Infinity and Love*

Since in Catholic theology charity is the "form" of all of the other virtues and that without which these latter easily

8. Cf. Delhaye's comment on the employment of this Augustinian phrase in the suppression of 'the idea of virtues and commandments in Philippe Delhaye, "La charité, 'premier commandement' chrétien chez S. Bonaventure," in *S. Bonaventura: 1274–1974*, vol. 4, *Theologica* (Grottaferrata, Italy: Collegio S. Bonaventura, 1974), 503–21, 504, 514–15.

9. Cf. Marx's problematic idea, described by von Balthasar, that the Mosaic law is better overcome by absorption "into the spontaneity of freedom" than by mere opposition; see Hans Urs von Balthasar, "Nine Theses in Christian Ethics," in *Readings in Moral Theology*, No. 2: *The Distinctiveness of Christian Ethics*, ed. Charles Curran and Richard McCormick, S.J. (New York and Ramsey, N.J.: Paulist Press, 1980), 190–206, 200.

degenerate into "splendid vices," the present description of virtue must be true of charity or else it is not true at all. In truth, virtue's not being defined by opposition is most evident in the case of love. It is often said that love has no upward limit. Whereas parameters are useful for identifying a virtue pedagogically, even a virtue such as temperance is not defined, strictly speaking, by the vices it avoids (here, overabstemiousness and gluttony). In the case of charity, parameters basically fail to have even a didactic function—and this is not only due to the abstract character of charity. Although love is certainly opposed to hatred and indifference, it is also quite intelligible without these notions and is not at all delineated over against an excess. By its limitless expansiveness alone, it bears a stronger resemblance than any other virtue to the absolute character of the true Infinite. Charity identifies the moral agent with his or her goal by means, likeness, and fruition in the beatific vision.

### *Dependence on the Finite*

We have just seen that virtue can be distorted and truncated by conceiving of it principally over against its opposite. We have also seen that true virtues, which do not admit of such a reduction, serve as catalysts for self-identification and maturation. Love manifests this power in an excelling way. In the next section of this chapter, we will locate this understanding of virtue, especially love, in the saving mediation of Christ. Before doing so, I will try to make the present point clear by enumerating other ways in which virtue fails to free itself sufficiently from its opposite. In the following cases, virtue is effectively understood only or primarily in relation to evil. By taking these as examples we should see that the attempt to live virtue first and foremost as nonviciousness is representative of a servile approach to Christian life.[10]

The first of such failures to consider is the twin problem of scrupulosity and legalism. Both are fixations on law for its own sake. While there is certainly nothing amiss in the careful observance of the dictates of nature and of divine positive commands, the feature that unites scrupulosity and legalism is a myopia that does not see the moral norm as illuminated by and as a conduit toward the love of God (in both the objective and subjective senses of the genitive).

Minimalism, similarly, considers moral norms only in the way of "duty" that should be dispensed with or dispensed of. Even the word *obligation,* which has less Enlightenment flavor than has "duty," is underpinned by similar notions of binding. Obligation may be the corollary of virtuous action informed by charity but never its essence. When, again, norms are reduced to binding or obligation (*ob-ligare*), they cannot be absolute (*ab-solvere*) and effective of transcendence. It is often pointed out that some notions of obligation are allied with deontological conceptions of the moral life. We do not need to labor the point that a morality in which the principal object is simply to respond without failing, to get the ball back over the net in every decision—rather than to move toward a personal end—will have disappointing results.

The final and perhaps most interesting example is the way

10. Cf. Jn 15:9–15, where love is central to the difference between servants and friends.

in which the conceptualization of moral norms in the way of borders or limitations often produces nothing more than a kind of obsession with that which stands on the other side of the limit. Fruit forbidden is, for this character, all the more delectable.[11] So also awareness of opposing vice and focus on the self (not the Thou) in practicing virtue intensify the desirability of whatever is prohibited. As soon as a person says to himself or herself, "Look how I am going without it!" he or she begins to want the thing foregone more intensely. The value that is transcendent and is the locus of transcendence for the person is virtually ignored, while limitation comes to occupy center stage in a manner that produces or increases concupiscence. When one loses sight of a value in favor of its threat, a value's protection can be taken as provocation.

## CHRIST "IN QUO OMNIA CONSTANT"

Grace[12] is the principle and root of virtue (but not virtue itself) for St. Thomas.[13] It is given by God, who is its principal efficient cause, through the humanity of Christ, which stands as its instrumental efficient cause.[14] The Council of Trent uses similar language about grace's fruit in justification.[15] The virtue

11. Cf. St. Thomas Aquinas, *In Epistolam II ad Corinthios,* 3, 2, as quoted in Philippe Delhaye, "La 'loi nouvelle' dans l'enseignement de S. Thomas," in *San Tommaso e la filosofia del diritto oggi: Saggi,* ed. Pontificia Accademia Romana di S. Tommaso (Rome: Pontificia Accademia Romana di S. Tommaso D'Aquino and Città Nuova Editrice, 1989), 73–103, 79: "Nam lex ... non reprimit concupiscentiam, sed magis occasionaliter auget, inquantum concupiscentia ferventius fertur in rem prohibitam." The locus classicus here is, naturally, Romans, for example, 7:7–11.

12. The paraphrase of Col 1:17 in the heading is from Maurice Blondel.

13. *ST* 1a2ae, 110, 3.

14. *ST* 1a2ae, 112, 1, ad 1m.

15. Council of Trent, Session 6, C. 7 (*Decrees of the Ecumenical Councils,*

in light of which persons are justified originates by the merit of the Passion. As lucid, powerful, and unassailable as these notions truly are—the divine power is the efficient cause of grace, the humanity of Christ is the instrumental efficient cause of grace, the Passion is the meritorious cause of justification—we may find that they leave very much still open. Seeking to follow up on these ideas does not, of course, mean setting them aside; it will be clear throughout the following as it has been in the foregoing that the traditional formulations have not been abandoned but continue to play an indispensable role.

The idea that God communicates the grace that effects virtue through the instrument of Christ's humanity bears further explanation. This notion, though true, does not include a description of the way in which it is true, whatever emphasis we rightly place on the meritorious character of the Passion. The Passion merits sanctifying grace (since it merits the justification that entails the virtues possessed in grace); yet we must here find an explanation for the fact that Christ is also the one Mediator between God and men.[16] While these notions are in no kind of contradiction, even at first glace, we must strive to see the mediatorship of Christ in its intrinsic relationship to the Passion; we do violence to both ideas when we see the Passion *only* as having merited the dispensation of mediating grace, as if by a merely arbitrary divine decree or fiat. The con-

2 vols., vol. 2, *Trent to Vatican II* [London and Washington, D.C.: Sheed & Ward and Georgetown University Press, 1990], 673–74); helpful here is Christopher J. Malloy, *Engrafted into Christ: A Critique of the Joint Declaration,* American University Studies, Series 7, Theology and Religion, Vol. 233 (New York: Peter Lang, 2005), esp. 25–26.

16. 1 Tm 2:5.

nection between mediatorship and Passion can appear to be external and somewhat mechanical without further explanation. Furthermore, understanding the Passion apart from other considerations risks accounting for the fact that grace is not simply *Gratia Dei* but *Gratia Christi* in a relatively superficial way. The question, then, is this: Grace has been earned by the Passion of Christ, but how has this grace been constituted and concretized in Christ? Grace is "of Christ" not merely because it is given because of him but because it is his.

In considering that the whole Trinity is the efficient cause of grace and salvation as such, and not the Son alone, our attention is drawn to the instrumental character of the humanity of the Son in Jesus' saving action on earth. Far from leaving us with an impoverished Christology, it is precisely this notion of instrumentality—together with the nonoppositional relationship of infinity to finitude that this entails—that opens up to us an important perspective on our sanctification in Christ. In this we see that Christ embodies and thus constitutes the free exercise of that human virtue which truly gives way to the Infinite and which bears the character of the true infinity toward which it strives. Christ's virtue is absolute or unbound both existentially—in that the actions that flow from it are free from evil—and essentially—in that its meaning bears an intrinsic relation to infinity.[17] This fact stands as the underpinning condition for the virtue of those who would be made members of Christ's body. Christ has not only merit-

17. This is implied, to give but a few examples, in Christ's being free from original sin (his lack of concupiscence is implied here), in his rejection of legalism, and in his focus on the divine will. See Mt 26:42; Lk 22:42; Jn 4:34, 5:30; Heb 10:7, 9; etc.

ed or earned that a gift, grace, should be bestowed; he himself seals and grounds the gift itself in his personal exercise of the virtue for which the gift exists. The meaning of grace is in the virtue that it sustains; virtue is realized—indeed, made real—in the concrete action of Christ. The attempt to account, however partially, for a connection between grace and the Passion must start with the premise that the Passion is meritorious not simply or principally because it was horrific, but because it was the consummation of Christ's virtue of love.[18]

In the previous chapter, we looked at Maurice Blondel's notion, already clearly present in his early (1893) *L'Action*, that the understanding of a Mediator would be constitutive of reality. The human knowing of Christ, in its passivity, allows finite, created realities to make themselves known. In making themselves known these things are established, in a new appropriation of the classical connection between being and intelligibility. Reality is constituted in its being known by a comprehensive, human intellect and in being reunited, in the Person of Christ, to the creative intellect of God.[19] In the Mediator, we find the finite thus rooted in the Infinite in a movement counter and complementary to the *Exitus* of creation.[20]

18. Cf. Karl Rahner, "The Body in the Order of Salvation," in *Theological Investigations,* vol. 17, trans. Margaret Kohl (New York: Crossroad, 1981), 71–89, 75–76.

19. Although we are focused in the immediate context on the role of the Mediator with respect to intelligible being, it is worth recalling that Blondel's thought is not limited to this. According to his insight Christ is capable of integrating (and redeeming) all things human—not only the will, action, etc.—but even sin. See, e.g., Maurice Blondel, *Action: Essay on a Critique of Life and a Science of Practice (1893),* trans. Oliva Blanchette (Notre Dame, Ind.: University of Notre Dame Press, 1984), 420–21, and René Marlé, S.J., ed., *Au coeur de la crise moderniste: Le dossier inédit d'une controverse* (Paris: Aubier, Éditions Montaigne, 1960), 79.

20. For a discussion of the thesis of Pierre Rousselot, S.J., that Christ grounds

Blondel makes an interesting, perhaps even compelling, case for Christ's being the constitutor of all things in his two natures. There is no difficulty in extending this (re)establishment of being to a grounding of the good—*Ens et bonum convertuntur* (Being and the good are convertible). Whatever doubts or confidences we may have in Blondel's striking claim, when so applied it fits elegantly with a classical understanding of human participation in divine charity. Christ's constitution of the good would not only apply to goods in the world but also to the human will that chooses those goods.

Each thing in the world receives its ultimate meaning in Christ in its own way—*Quidquid recipitur per modum recipientis recipitur* (Whatever is received is received in the way of the receiver). Even subrational things, which cannot deliberately pursue God as their end, are dignified by the fact of the Incarnation. Christ's everyday human interaction with the natural world, in incorporating its objects in his own voluntary life, confers a new significance on this order for those persons who live in the world as members of his body. Particular ends (and actions) are saturated with sense in having been elected and engaged by the Incarnate Word. While the natural world does not become supernatural per se, it ennobled with the capacity of being subordinated to the pursuit of God as the object of supernatural beatitude. The presence of this end redounds in significance to the concrete action that engages the world. Persons achieve a supernatural end by Christ and

the conceptual order, see especially John McDermott, S.J., *Love and Understanding: The Relation of Will and Intellect in Pierre Rousselot's Christological Vision,* Analecta Gregoriana, 229, B, 77 (Rome: Università Gregoriana Editrice, 1983), 260–65.

are received into Christ who, by his own historical action, has already mediated natural actions to an infinite finality in supernatural love. Actions on the way to the supernatural end are, *eo ipso,* in the Way. Human actions in the world are not linked by simple fiat to a supernatural end; rather, action and end are intrinsically connected through the mediation of Christ Crucified. By a human will hypostatically united to the Infinite, Christ grounds goods and their election in action, bringing them across the chasm between finite and Infinite and rooting them in abysmal goodness. By his human intellect, according to Blondel, Christ receives the intelligibility of the natural world and solidifies it in establishing a return of this intelligibility to its source in the creative intellect of God. So also, by his human will, Christ is the instrument for the renewal and elevation of creation in enfolding the finite in the infinity of divine love.

The one Mediator loves a reality that is given a new destiny by this very fact and made commensurate with an eschatological glorification. The material world, with its nexus of conscious and unconscious relations, becomes the theater for persons' supernatural attainment of Love because Love has first loved it.

Grace is not given on the occasion of the Cross; it is, instead, the blood of Love that falls from the Cross. Had Christ not perfected (in every sense of this word) human virtue, human persons would have no way to possess its fullness and the salvation to which this leads.

[ 4 ]

# *ESSE SECUNDARIUM*

In the preceding chapter, we looked at the way in which Christ unites the finite and the mutable with the Infinite and the stable by his voluntary acts. This discussion was naturally preceded by a look at Christ's knowledge of the reality that he would redeem. The union of the finite and the Infinite that is the concrete form of redemption is realized through the passivity of human knowing and the activity of choosing. At this point it seems appropriate to press the question of whether the Infinite and the finite are united in Christ in any other way. Scholastic theology raised this issue, without drawing out all of its implications, when it asked whether Christ's being is one only—divine and uncreated being—or not.[1] Is the being that enacts the created nature of Christ nothing other than

1. A good overview of terms and thinkers operative in the question of Christ's *Esse* from St. Thomas to post-Tridentine theology can be found in Adam, *The Christ of Faith,* 192–204.

the being of the Second Person of the Trinity? St. Thomas, according to common (not unanimous) opinion, held to the singularity of Christ's being until near to the end of his life. In a disputed question he suggests that created and "secondary" being (*Esse secundarium*) corresponds to Christ's human nature. While it remains true for St. Thomas even here that one uncreated and substantial being is the Incarnate Word's *simpliciter,* his earlier notion that no other (created) belongs to the humanity of Christ has been nuanced in an important way. In Christ there is created, nonpersonal, and dependent being that is not, for all of that, properly accidental.[2]

St. Thomas offers in light adumbration what amounts to a ponderous qualification of both Christology and metaphysics. Before investigating the import of this shift, I would simply remark that perhaps St. Thomas is closer here to the position that Duns Scotus would espouse than many authors have recognized. Although Scotus speaks deliberately and freely of "double being" (*Duplex esse*)—created and uncreated—in Christ, he is willing to acknowledge that Christ only exists formally and simply by one of these beings. Created being, for him, stands in respect to this being somewhat as would

2. See St. Thomas Aquinas, *Quaestiones disputatae et quaestiones duodecim quodlibetales,* 7th ed., vol. 2 (Rome: Domus Editorialis Marietti Taurini, 1942), 481: *De unione Verbi incarnati,* Art. 4: "In Christo autem suppositum subsistens est persona Filii Dei, quae simpliciter substantificatur per naturam divinam, non autem simpliciter substantificatur per naturam humanam; quia persona Filii Dei fuit ante humanitatem assumptam ... et ideo sicut Christus est unum simpliciter propter unitatem suppositi, et duo secundum quid propter duas naturas; ita habet unum esse simpliciter propter unum esse aeternum aeterni suppositi. Est autem et aliud esse hujus suppositi, non in quantum est aeternum, sed in quantum est temporaliter homo factum; quod esse etsi non sit esse accidentale, quia homo non praedicatur accidentaliter de Filio Dei ... non tamen est esse principale sui suppositi, sed secundarium."

an accident.[3] The prima facie similarity between Scotus and Thomas on this point does not, however, minimize the stark distinction between Christ's two beings in Scotus or obliterate the difference between his thought and that of Thomas.[4]

That such a shift occurred in St. Thomas's position is not entirely uncontested by scholars.[5] Moreover, even among those Thomists who concede that the disputed question represents a substantial revision in St. Thomas's thought, a few earnestly

3. John Duns Scotus, *Opera Omnia,* vol. 20, *Lectura in Librum Tertium Sententiarum* (Vatican City: Typis Vaticanis, 1950), 169–83: *Lectura* 3, Dist. 6, Q. 1. See lines 219–22 (179) in particular: "Cum ... natura [creata] adveniat Verbo in esse suppositi constituto, et se habeat ad Verbum quodammodo sicut accidens ad subiectum, sequitur quod licet in Christo sint plura esse, tamen in ipso est tantum unum esse quo formaliter exsistit." Scotus argues forcefully in this question against the singularity of Christ's *Esse.* For other arguments to the same point, see Diepen, *L'Emmanuel,* esp. 102–26. For more on Diepen's view, over against the model of absolute singularity of being (which he characteristically terms the "ecstasy of being" position), see esp. 143–58, in which one of the objectives is to separate St. Thomas's thought from that of Scotus. Cf. 18, 24–26, 61–64, and 66–67, which take up the question of the unity of God's causality in relation to the being of Christ. Cf. also 68, which suggests that Maritain's consideration of *Esse secundarium* on the analogy of an accident puts him, *volens nolens,* among the supporters of *Duplex esse.*

4. Many sources have proved helpful in gaining a foothold in Scotus's thought here; given the scope of the present chapter, only one may be mentioned: Zachary Hayes, O.F.M., "The Plurality of *Esse* in Christ According to Matthew of Aquasparta," in *Essays Honoring Allan B. Wolter,* ed. William A. Frank and Girard J. Etzkorn (St. Bonaventure, N.Y.: Franciscan Institute of St. Bonaventure University, 1985).

5. See, e.g., Deloffre's introduction to St. Thomas Aquinas, *Question disputée l'union du Verbe incarné (De unione Verbi incarnati),* trans. Marie-Hélène Deloffre (Paris: Librairie Philosophique J. Vrin, 2000), 22–23. Delhoffre supplies an excellent overview of this debate on 13–23. Cf. Henk J. M. Schoot, "The Ineffable Being of Christ According to Thomas Aquinas," in *Atti del IX Congresso tomistico internazionale, 5: Problemi teologici alla luce dell'Aquinate,* ed. Antonio Piolanti, Studi Tomistici, 44 (Vatican City: Libreria Editrice Vaticana, 1991). Although Schoot does not call into question Thomas's authorship of *De unione Verbi incarnati,* he nevertheless does not believe that Thomas changed his mind on the being of Christ.

deny that St. Thomas, in writing it, was true to his own principles.[6]

I believe that the position that I take to be Thomas's final thought on the question of Christ's being, that presented in *De unione Verbi incarnati,* represents an improvement over his earlier answers to this question. If it can be shown that the notion of *Esse secundarium* is consistent with other theological principles, largely drawn from St. Thomas's own thought, then we will find ourselves in a better position to consider what this view offers to the understanding of Christ as Mediator that I have tried to suggest. Christ's mission of course defies any neat formulation, but one of the ways that we have approached this mission, especially in the last chapter, has been in terms of a reconciliation of the finite and the Infinite. In the first two chapters of this book, I sought to highlight the desirability of holding closely together Jesus' identity and mission, such that our conceptions of these are reciprocally defining. Is there a way to root this fundamental understanding

6. See, e.g., Albert Patfoort, "L'Enseignement de saint Thomas sur l''esse' du Christ," in *Problèmes actuels de christologie,* ed. Humbert Bouëssé and Jean-Jacques Latour, Textes et études théologiques (Paris: Desclée de Brouwer, 1965). Perhaps in regret that Thomas adopted the language of secondary being, other thinkers try to minimize its impact. Corvez may be thinking along these lines when he writes: "Il semble que nous ayons ainsi exorcisé le mythe de l'*esse* secondaire conçu à la manière d'un acte, qui n'est pas l'acte d'être ou l'esse pur et simple, mais un acte reçu dans l'essence par participation de l'*Esse* en tant qu'il actue cette essence. L'essence est acte par elle-même, acte en puissance à l'existence.... Sous l'*esse,* avec lui, en union intrinsèque avec lui, il n'y a qu'une puissance réelle, qui, par l'*esse,* cause formelle de l'existant, est devenue réelle d'une réalité existante"; see M. Corvez, O.P., "La 'distinction réelle' et l'unicité de l'être dans le Christ," *Revue Thomiste* 59 (1959): 704–15, 711; also see 710–11 et passim. Cf. Bernard Lonergan, S.J., *The Ontological and Psychological Constitution of Christ,* trans. Michael G. Shields, *Collected Words of Bernard Lonergan,* vol. 7 (Toronto, Buffalo, N.Y., and London: University of Toronto Press, 2002), 144/45–150/51.

of Jesus' mission—the reconciliation of the finite and the Infinite—in his basic identity as the Incarnate Word? We must be cautious in doing so for two reasons. In the first place, created being, as such, is not a "thing" that falls; "finite" and "fallen" are not functionally interchangeable terms. Second, we must constantly remind ourselves, especially in light of Vatican I's *Dei Filius,* that God is free with respect to the created order. He is not bound to save; still less is he bound to save in such-and-such a way. Bearing the first point in mind, it is not out of place to observe that the created, finite order is de facto a fallen order. Finite being is not a thing that has fallen; but all things that have fallen are finite.[7] With respect to the second consideration, although God could have saved in any way or none at all, he evidently did desire to save and this in an entirely fitting way: we cannot be perplexed to find that Jesus is suited to his mission not only in the means at his disposal but also in his identity. It is not just that Jesus has the wherewithal to save; he is the Savior. We should try to conceive of this on the most fundamental level possible. No one denies that Jesus has a limited nature, but let us follow this fact out in its implications. Does it suggest that Jesus has, at a level more formal than nature, a thoroughgoing solidarity with the finite order?

The proliferation of literature devoted to the *Esse secundarium* question in the middle part of the twentieth century corresponds in measure to its notorious difficulty.[8] I do not pre-

7. Although the point here pushes in the direction of eschatology, I would like to be clear that I intend this along the lines of Rm 8:22 and not at all of ἀποκατάστασις πάντων.

8. Cf. John McDermott, S.J., "The Christologies of Karl Rahner, II," *Gregorianum* 67, no. 2 (1986): 297–327, 309–10: "[T]he question of the number of existences in Christ Himself [is] a question that bedeviled not only modern Thomists

tend to offer an easy or complete answer here. I would like to begin by cursorily proposing several difficulties with the notion that the Word, in the divine Being that he is, can be said to provide the ontological foundation for the human nature of Christ without any further qualification, that is, that there is simply and only one being in Christ.

In the first place, to maintain that in Christ the being of the Word is the being that enacts his human nature seems to court pantheism. Divine Being is equivalent to the divine Form. A nature that receives infinite, Subsisting Being Itself as Itself, *eo ipso* receives the divine Essence.[9] We really only have two examples of reception of the divine Essence: the filiation of the Son from the Father and the spiration of the Holy Spirit from the Father and the Son together. These are obviously inner-Trinitarian processions, the recipients of which are fully divine and uncreated. The created nature of the Son must be enacted by being that is not identical with the Essence of God in order for Christ's humanity to remain human and for there to be a true distinction between Christ's natures. To hold that Christ's humanity could remain itself while receiving the divine Being/Nature is implicitly to denature divinity. It is not possible to conceive of one nature receiving another distinct, substantial nature.

Since the divine Essence cannot be denatured or changed,

but also St. Thomas himself. On the one hand, it is difficult to see how a finite nature can receive an infinite act of existence utterly out of proportion to itself. On the other hand, ascribing a subordinate, finite *esse* to Christ leads to a conundrum; either the finite *esse* introduces an ultimate duality in activity and a possible opposition to the divine *Esse* or its total subjugation to the divine *Esse* renders it superfluous. However insoluble this problem seems, a Thomist must face it."

9. Adrian Hastings, "Christ's Act of Existence," *Downside Review* 73, no. 232 (1955): 139–59, 154–55, makes a similar argument concerning pantheism.

when we talk about a created form we do not suggest that it is restriction of or parceling from Uncreated Being. Created form is the restriction or concretion of being,[10] but it cannot be the restriction of illimitable being.[11] We can readily see that finitized, Infinite Being would be a contradiction in terms, but is anything other than this required to maintain the absolute singularity of Christ's being? If, on the other hand, we hold in some way that Jesus' humanity is actualized by created being, we do not encounter this problem since created being is not essentially infinite.

Another difficulty with the "ecstasy of being" model calls our attention back to the rule that God's action with respect to creation is undivided. The lack of any created being in Christ would render unintelligible the idea that the whole Trinity creates the human nature of Christ (while this nature is united to the Son alone).[12] Since creation is an *Opus ad extra,* it must be common to the Trinitarian Persons. How does the whole Trinity create, if not by "supplying" being to that which is created? In the absence of created being, the actuator of the humanity of Christ would be the Son alone.[13] One may object that the

10. In chapter 1 we discussed how nature concretizes person, but we must be attentive to the difference between these "concretizations," since person is not equivalent to being. For the latter point, see Luigi (Aloysius) Ciappi, "De unitate Ontologica ac Psychologica Personae Christi," *Angelicum* 29 (1952): 182–89, 186–87, and Réginald Garrigou-Lagrange, O.P., "L'unique personnalité du Christ," *Angelicum* 29 (1952): 60–75, 72–73.

11. Cf. Corvez, "La 'Distinction Réelle'," 708–10 et passim, which raises this problem but responds to it with the curious answer that Jesus' human nature, as created—with such-and-such meaning and parameters—by the undivided Trinity, limits itself. It contains its own reality and meaning as created; that is, it is not really a restriction of divine *Esse.*

12. See *ST* 3, 3, 2; 3, 3, 4 on the principle and term of assumption. See 3, 2, 7 on the created union and created nature.

13. Cf. Antonio Piolanti, "L'Essere del Verbo Incarnato," *Divinitas* 3 (1959):

Being or Act of the Son is inner-Trinitarian, but this does not dissolve the fact that precisely external work is at issue here. It is, similarly, not helpful to suggest that we are not dealing here with a case of efficient causality—since the humanity of Jesus is manifestly not God—or to employ the model of formal causality as a substitute—for such would be to misunderstand or misrepresent the meaning of this type of causality.

A final consideration brings us again to the subject of Christ's true humanity. The human soul or form is that by which being (with meaning) is "transmitted" to the matter that is formed into the body.[14] God enacts the person and it is in and by his soul that the person enacts the matter formed to be the body. The Person of Christ, too, by his human soul communicates being and intelligibility to the matter of his body.[15] In enacting his human body, the Son of God, as divine, works through secondary causality; the Son of God, as human, works as a secondary cause. Here is the catch: if created being is in no sense in Christ, then we must suppose that divine Being, the *Causa causarum,* is deployed by a secondary cause.[16] Yet, if we do not admit that Christ's soul is communicative of being to the matter of his body, we call into question the integrity of his human nature.

The Word Incarnate humanly mediates created act. He

---

77–94, 92: "La natura umana di Cristo fu tratta dal nulla, è quindi creata. Ma fu creata non per l'unione a un atto di essere creato, ma per l'unione *in tempore* all'atto di essere increato dal Verbo di Dio.... [P]er uscire dal nulla [non] si richiede sempre un atto di essere creato."

14. *ST* 1, 75, 6; 76, 1; 76, 4; 3, 17, 2, ad 4m; etc.

15. See *ST* 3, 6, 1.

16. Cf., however, *ST* 3, 17, 2, Obj. 4 and ad 4m. Thomas's concern here will be tacitly addressed in the following.

receives this act from the whole Trinity. Do we only risk still greater difficulties with this solution? Can we say that the Word Incarnate alone mediates being while the whole Trinity gives being to his nature? Can we likewise separate the enhypostatization of the human nature of Christ from the creation of that nature, such that the former can belong to one Person alone while the latter belongs to the whole Trinity? All of this is only to take the basic facts of the Incarnation seriously. Jesus shares the reception of being from the Trinity with every human being. Human persons give (to the matter of their bodies) being that is theirs but is not of their own origination. There is no reason why a divine Person cannot communicate being that is not of his sole origination. Moreover, such mediation of created being in the Incarnation is not a violation of rule that divine actions in the created order are Trinitarian and not unique to individual divine Persons. The reason for this is that the reception and mediation of being is a purely human act, quite unlike the act of creation itself.[17]

In pointing to problems with the theory in which Christ has no created being that corresponds to his humanity, it is crucially important not to risk the opposite extreme. The finite, secondary being of Christ is not the being that pertains to substance, even if it is not that which pertains to accidents either.[18] Both of these extremes—understanding the created being of Christ as his substantial being *simpliciter* or as accidental—are to be rejected for fairly obvious and often repeat-

17. A fuller account of human, proper acts and common, divine acts of the Word is given in chapter 1.

18. Cf. *ST* 1, 76, 4, ad 4m.

ed reasons.[19] We can say neither that a conjoined nature has independent, stand-alone existence nor that Christ's humanity is accidental to his divine Substance.[20] Some have argued that *Esse secundarium* should be considered as a sui generis case in metaphysics, since there is simply no other example of being that is neither substantial nor accidental.

Because of the uniqueness of secondary being, we may find that it is vastly more difficult to say what it is than to say what it is not. Explaining *what* being is, however, is really the wrong errand. We can say what essences are, because essences are whatnesses, but in the case of being we must be content to describe how it works and what its limits are. With this in mind, I would offer five considerations in summary fashion: (1) The being that pertains to the humanity of Christ is efficiently caused by the undivided Trinity.[21] (2) The position of secondary being with respect to the infinite Being of the Word belongs to its very creation and constitution; the Word does not perform a unique and particular work in sustaining secondary being. (3) Yet this being does not stand apart; it is perfectly embedded in the *Esse simpliciter* of the Word. (4) It does not for this fact alter or supplement in any sense the Word's divine Being. (5) Although it does not stand apart, *Esse secundarium* underpins a reality of its own order.

I have done little more here than suggest parameters within which further thought about Christ's being may be productive.

19. Cf. St. Thomas Aquinas, *Verbe incarné,* 64–67, in which Deloffre offers a valuable discussion of Thomas's use of these terms vis-à-vis the being of Christ.

20. *ST* 3, 2, 6.

21. Language is, of course, limited here. We should not conceive of being as stand-alone stuff that is superadded to a created form.

Why is this an important question and what is its relevance to the present study? In previous chapters I maintained that the infinite Person of Christ internalizes the finite order. In chapter 1, we saw that Christ understands himself as divine in his redemptive role. He does not truly and fully understand himself as Redeemer unless he understands those whom he redeems. In chapter 2, I tried to show on a deeper level that Jesus' consciousness and self-understanding are identified with—even in some sense constituted by—the other human consciousnesses and self-understandings that occupy a capital position in the finite and fallen world. Chapter 3 extended and completed this line of thought since, unless Christ unites that which he knows to infinite Love by truly human acts of love, there can be no transformation of these beings in their freedom. The question of Christ's love urges us on to consider the distillation of this love in human affectivity, apart from which Christ is hardly a *human* redeemer. We will turn to this issue in chapter 5; however something more had to be said at this point about the unification of the finite and infinite orders in a most basic way, that is, at the level of Christ's ontological constitution. By arguing against the "ecstasy of being" modeling of this constitution and in favor of the notion of *Esse secundarium,* I have sought to show that Christ is himself, in one Person, the integration of finite and infinite Being. He is the living bridge between holy Infinity and the finite order, even in the latter's deficiency in sin and evil. That which Christ does is rooted in that which he is. Such and so great a Redeemer[22] as we have stands the finite within himself in redeeming the fallen world.

22. The paraphrase is, of course, from the *Exultet.*

[ 5 ]

# THE ANGER OF CHRIST

At the end of the last chapter, I suggested that an account of Jesus' emotional life is essential in picturing his full humanity. Love in human life is accompanied by feelings and sentiments. Our concern with the Lord's affective life, however, involves much more than acknowledging his integral humanity, as if arguing—wisely, no doubt—in the following way: human beings have emotions, Jesus was a human being, therefore Jesus had emotions. Rather, we can see Christ's emotions in a soteriological context.

Of Christ's emotions, perhaps the most unlikely possibility for a part in redemption is his anger. When we think about Christ's affective life, features such as his compassion, his mercy, his desire to be close to his disciples, and other like sentiments sit very well with us. They are quite easy to attribute to Jesus. When Jesus expresses, from his depths, a longing to gather Jerusalem like a mother hen;[1] when Jesus tells his disciples that he has earnestly desired to celebrate a meal with them;[2] when Jesus allows the disciple whom he loved to recline against his chest,[3] we know that we are in the presence of someone who loves affectively and passionately. This is disquieting, because of our "guilty frigidity,"[4] even as it gives a great sense of security and trust.

When, however, Jesus drives the sellers from the Temple;[5] when he calls Simon Peter a satan;[6] when he vehemently castigates scribes and Pharisees,[7] we find ourselves somewhat thrown off balance. Perhaps we are even vaguely embarrassed by Jesus' anger. In response, we often try to explain these scenes away or minimize their presence in the life story of Jesus. How often, indeed, do these scenes from Scripture make it into our art and literature?

I have absolutely no wish to minimize, in my own turn, Jesus' open benevolence in the Gospels or in Christian experience of the Savior as reflected in writing, prayer, and ecclesial life. In focusing on Jesus' anger I would like to suggest, if only by extension, that all of his emotions are intrinsically connected to salvation. Far from being an embarrassment, Christ's anger is a particularly apt case for showing this; this feeling represents, from one particular perspective, the leading edge of his emotive life.

The Church Fathers and the medievals, historians point

1. Mt 23.37 and Lk 13:34.
2. Lk 22:15.
3. Jn 13:23–25.
4. The phrase belongs to von Balthasar, *Love Alone,* 51.
5. Mt 21:12–13, Mk 11:15–17, Lk 19:45–46, and Jn 2:14–17.
6. Mt 16:23 and Mk 8:33.
7. E.g., Mt 23:1–36 and par.

out, often dealt with the subject of Christ's anger in the spirit of defending his sinlessness. They often characterized his anger as a "propassion," that is, a passion that does not go so far in its movements or effects as to occasion a sinful volition on Christ's part or to cloud his reason. True and important as the insight is here, we must see in this treatment a purely defensive move. This account does not yet say something positive about Jesus' anger; it only tells us what this emotion cannot mean. Similarly, we can see that it contributes to our understanding the humanity of Christ, but it does not yet speak directly to his human involvement in salvation. To an even greater degree today, the subject of Christ's anger is placed in a very limited context. We err when we try to excuse expressions of Christ's anger as occasional outbursts, brought on by understandable frustrations, stress, and so on. Such characterizations push Christ's anger to the sidelines of his identity.

The anger of Jesus is at the heart of his salvific mission, just as is his compassion. We could not easily say this unless the one emotion were the flipside of the other. To make this point clear, we must cleanly separate Jesus' anger from irritability, pugnacity, simple impatience, and the like. To propose such a separation seems to suggest that I intend to continue thinking of this question within perspectives just mentioned, that is, that I intend to show that Jesus' anger does not represent a character flaw and, more to the point, is not morally wrong.[8] Instead, I will take this point as given for the moment. However, if it does become clear in the course of our discussion

8. Texts such as Mt 18:23–35, Mt 22:2–14, and Lk 14:15–24, and Eph 4:26 would help to make such a point.

that Jesus' human feelings of anger—along with the acts to which these feelings contribute—have a soteriological significance, it will be evident, a fortiori, that his anger is not sinful.

We must be on guard against a compartmentalization of Jesus' life, such that his Crucifixion and Resurrection are understood in connection with salvation while the other events of his life are not. No doubt Crucifixion and Resurrection are principally salvific, but the personality, accomplishments, history, and so on of the one who goes to the Cross are not simply incidentals that can be omitted from our theology. No doubt we begin to overcome this problem when we consider along narrative lines the events that led to Jesus' execution[9] or the impact that his teaching had on his disciples in the light of the Resurrection. Yet we seldom consider the emotions of Jesus as a kind of color indicator of his mission, as driving toward and consummated in his death.

Perhaps our usual assumptions are not so categorically excluding, however. It may be the case that we do not wish to deny *all* of Christ's emotions the dignity of being relevant to salvation. It may be that some emotions are quite readily seen as important. If pressed on the point, we would be loath to set aside Christ's healings, mercy, compassion, or even his friendships as extraneous to his true purpose. Is Jesus' rage one thing—perhaps the only thing—that doesn't really fit into the picture of his identity as Savior?

Perhaps we are willing to go one step further. We may assume that the Lord battled evil with anger during his life, in some salvific sense, but dealt with it entirely contrariwise in

9. In reference, e.g., to Mk 11:18.

his death. Christ's death was the event—so it would seem—of others' anger toward him rather than of Christ's own, by then certainly extinguished, anger. This also is a strange assumption.

The contrary of this assumption is that the Cross represents the consummation of Jesus' anger. This claim looks no less strange, though, in light of New Testament perspectives on the Passion.[10] What sort of anger is expressed in *bearing* violence?

Before forming any judgment on this issue, to which we will return at the end of this reflection, we should look at the phenomenon of anger itself. In some sense, anger comes very close to sorrow. Anger and sorrow are distinguished most significantly by the possibility or impossibility of redress. The bitterness of sorrow is futility. Nothing can be done to right the evil at the source of sorrow; it must simply be suffered. This is not to say that sorrow cannot eventually give rise to action,[11] but action does not immediately flow from sorrow as such. Like sorrow, anger is a response to evil; however, anger is active in its regard and is focused directly against it in the mode of vindication, elimination, or overcoming. Anger is an emotion that spurs a person to act. (The questions of whether this emotion is heeded or not, of whether or not acting would be successful, etc. do not impact this characterization. Similarly, the fact that anger can linger after the possibility of acting has passed does not change its essential orientation.) Sorrow does not directly incite action.[12] One's emotional reaction to the false accusation of a close friend, for example, would not

10. Cf., e.g., the use of Is 53:7 in Acts 8:32.
11. See, e.g., *ST* 2a2ae, 30, 1.
12. Thomas takes this up in *ST* 1a2ae, 46, 1.

primarily consist in sorrow but a in relentless and holy fury in the service of vindication, at least while there remains an expectation of righting the wrong. This example also illustrates the fact that anger is not directed only toward the restoration of justice in one's own case. Love seeks good for the beloved.[13] Where the beloved is deprived of the good intended for him or her in love—that is, when the beloved suffers or perpetrates evil—love is displayed in anger.[14]

We may think of Christ's anger with respect to physical and moral evils (*Mala poenae* and *Mala culpae*), given their organic connection, as of a piece. The forceful Calvinist scholar of a century ago, B. B. Warfield, illustrates this point very nicely in a chapter dedicated to the theme of Jesus' emotions.[15] Following F. Gumlich and others, Warfield suggests that the central emotion of Christ at Lazarus's tomb is not sorrow but anger. He argues this point by observing that in describing Jesus' emotional state, the word used—and used twice, which suggests its pivotal place in the story—is ἐμβριμάομαι, which betokens anger and indignation. His interpretation goes against

13. Traces of this classical formulation of love can still be found, in spite of today's well-noted sentimentalization of love. For example, "I love you" is most commonly expressed in Italian with the phrase "Ti voglio bene," which is, very literally, "I want good for you."

14. Although concupiscence is not to be confused with charity, Thomas's insight into the former's relation to irascibility is foundational for the present discussion; see *ST* 1, 81, 2, and, for his notion of love's relation to the passions in general, 1a2ae, 27, 4.

15. Benjamin Breckinridge Warfield, *The Person and Work of Christ* (Philadelphia: Presbyterian and Reformed Publishing Company, 1950), 91–145; see esp. 107–22 for Warfield's engaging treatment of Jesus' anger in the Gospels. Another valuable exposition of Jesus' anger, from the point of view of St. Thomas, is Paul Gondreau, *The Passions of Christ's Soul in the Theology of St. Thomas Aquinas* (Münster: Aschendorff Verlag GmbH & Co, 2002), 427–41. Cf. 37, note 7, for a list of evangelical references to Jesus' anger.

our natural assumptions when reading this scene, but Warfield is worth hearing out:

> Inextinguishable fury seizes upon him; his whole being is discomposed and perturbed; and his heart, if not his lips, cries out—"For the innumerable dead / Is my soul disquieted." It is death that is the object of his wrath, and behind death him who has the power of death, and whom he has come into the world to destroy. Tears of sympathy may fill his eyes, but this is incidental. His soul is held by rage.... The raising of Lazarus thus becomes, not an isolated marvel, but ... a decisive instance and open symbol of Jesus' conquest of death and hell. What John does for us in this particular statement is to uncover to us the heart of Jesus, as he wins for us our salvation. Not in cold unconcern, but in flaming wrath against the foe, Jesus smites in our behalf.[16]

Warfield brilliantly captures the movement of anger toward the restoration of life and goodness. Yet our application of anger to Christ seems already to push anger beyond its most basic and elemental meaning. We saw in passing above that anger gives rise, most evidently, to the restoration of justice. St. Thomas is representative of a long tradition that sees anger in this light.[17] In anger one seeks to restore that which is due but not possessed. In this way, anger would have a place apart from our present and imperative call to the supernatural charity that outstrips the claims of simple justice. However—without prejudice to the undeniable truth of this connection between anger and mere justice—it is difficult for us to see anger as properly salvific in this context alone. Christ, it will

16. Warfield, *Person and Work,* 117. Warfield's discussion of the raising of Lazarus is found on 114–17. The internal reference is to a poem by John Greenleaf Whittier, "The Grave by the Lake."

17. *ST* 2a2ae, 158, 1.

count as a truism to say, is intrinsically supernatural. What I mean by this is not simply that he is God but that his human nature is structured in intrinsic openness to supernatural fulfillment. An apparent deviation from our path here will put us straight upon it: the sacred humanity of Christ is *the* counterexample that brings up short any claim that God could not create a nature that does not bear within itself the principles of its own fulfillment since, allegedly, to do so would be to posit a natural claim on grace. The human nature of Christ is and remains, Chalcedon reminds us, of the natural order. Yet it is nothing without the grace of union in the Incarnation.[18] In the present economy of salvation, Christ's humanity is the archetype for nature that has no complete sufficiency and no final fulfillment on its own terms, that is to say, Christ's humanity is the template for human indigence of a supernatural complement. The point here is not directly to criticize an argument in favor of the "two-ends" solution to the problem of nature and grace but rather to suggest that in Christ, just as nature is not a self-contained and self-sufficient reality, so also the anger that serves justice is not a purely natural or justice-bound emotion. Charity has its own law and its own logic, which defy transgression. Zealous for his Father's house, Jesus renders to his Father his due, but this is inconceivable purely on the plane of the commutative relationships, economics (in the broad sense), and so on that characterize justice in itself.

In fact, we find everything about Jesus hard to place be-

18. To object here that the divine Person "antedates" the humanity of Christ in order to imply that the cases of Incarnation and the bestowal of grace on human persons differ is to overlook the fact the divine intention of bestowing grace is also prior to the real existences of human beings.

cause nothing of him fits within the common, natural world. Jesus' kingship in John's Gospel offers an excellent illustration of this point. The Pilate of John's Gospel repeatedly mocks the kingship of Christ. At the same time, paradoxically, he plaintively and pathetically holds out Christ's kingship (and his lampoon thereof) to the Jews as grounds for exculpating Christ. The prefect seems obsessed with the kingship of Christ, as if there is something in this at once familiar and unrecognizable. His discomfiture with Jesus' claim to be king stems in part from Jesus' demurral from kingship as Pilate understands it.[19] In the face of this, Pilate exemplifies the human temptation to reduce all realities to familiar, human terms. The common denominator between Pilate's story and ours is that the supernatural puts us ill at ease no less than the unnatural. We who read Gospel stories of Christ's anger also find ourselves somewhat at a loss. In Christ, the lucid intelligibility of justice becomes the reflecting screen for the radiant mystery of charity and the cold calculation of vindication becomes the searing fury of God's human love.

Christ's anger, like the scandalous Cross itself, cannot be plotted with our coordinates. Just as it calls for a complete reorientation on the part of the one receiving its force, his anger calls for nothing less on the part of the person hearing or reading about it. Thus, acknowledging the mysterious and

19. Yet does Pilate begin to perceive the challenge that Jesus presents to his own notions of kingship? Are these notions thrown into question, such that their hold on him begins to loosen? Jesus' accusers must repeatedly remind Pilate of the implications and obligations of regal authority, while Pilate, in Jesus' presence, begins to display an insouciant, even cavalier, attitude toward intramundane power. Cf. Jn 18:31, 19:12, 15.

complex character of this emotion in Christ is, perhaps, a first step toward appreciating its significance. Peter Chrysologus alludes to the fundamental complexity of Jesus' emotions in commenting on Christ's healing of the man with a withered hand as this story appears in Mark's Gospel. (It is worth noting that, while all of the Synoptics recount this episode, only Mark includes the detail that Jesus, disturbed, looked around with anger before effecting the cure.)[20] In reference to Mark's text, Chrysologus says:

> "Looking over," it says, not "looking," that is, not merely gazing at an appearance as a man does, but as God contemplating bodies, hearts, minds, feelings, the past, the present, and the future. *Looking them over with anger, he was saddened.* He was angry as the Lord, saddened as a parent, sorrowing as a man, seeing as God.[21]

Though he is truly man, there is something in Christ's human feelings of anger that cannot simply be likened to or measured by ordinary human experience.

Christ seeks to restore the balance of justice *flagello iracundiae suae* (by the whip of his anger), in the apt phrase of Rupert of Deutz;[22] he seeks to punish sinners as restitution

20. Cf. Mk 3:1–6 with Mt 12:9–14 and Lk 6:6–11.

21. "Circumspiciens dixit, non conspiciens, id est, non tantum faciem ut homo intuens, sed ut Deus corpora, corda, mentes, sensus, præterita, præsentia, futura contemplatus. *Circumspiciens eos cum ira, contristatus.* Irascitur ut dominus, contristatur ut parens, dolet ut homo, intuetur ut Deus"; see Petrus Chrysologus [Peter Chrysologus], *Sermo XXXII: De eo qui habebat manum aridam* in *Opera Omnia in Patrologiae cursus completus,* vol. 52, Patrologia Latina (Paris: J.-P. Migne, 1846), 291. The editorial note that corresponds to this text in Migne clarifies "irascitur" and "contristatur" in a thoroughly insightful way: "Non erat ira Christi appetitio vindictæ, sed indignatio in vitia: et contristabatur de peccatis, sed ut parens miseretur filiorum peccantium."

22. Rupertus Abbas Tuitiensis [Rupert of Deutz], *Commentaria in Apocalypsim*

to God of his due. Yet within this movement—indeed, at the heart of it—Christ seeks to restore the human person to himself or herself as the pinnacle of the material order governed by justice sublated to charity. Christ's anger, then, does not restore justice simply, as would assertion against an enemy. God's method of restoring justice involves, but is in no way exhausted by, an ire that effects a personal relationship and purifies this in love. By his anger Jesus burns his way into the human heart. Usually we think of finding a way into another's heart by means of affection, but the heart's door can also be opened by anger. Anger and affection turn the common key of openness and vulnerability.

The vulnerability of the human person before God is a sign and condition of strength and not of weakness.[23] In a noteworthy meditation on Jacob's fight with the "man" in Gn 32, Jean-Louis Chrétien urges the point that blessing is precisely in the wound that one receives from the divine. In conversation with Rainer Maria Rilke (in the poem "*Der Schauende*"), the seventeenth-century Dominican Louis Chardon, and others, Chrétien sees human greatness in the person's being accosted and bested by God. Where the human person wins trivial triumphs, he or she is reduced to this proportion. Where instead one succumbs to the force of the divine challenger and leans in injury on God, one becomes stronger. In this light we see again that Christ's criticisms and rebukes in the Gospels are directed, not only toward the restoration of

---

*Joannis Apostoli* in *Patrologiae cursus completus,* vol. 169, Patrologia Latina (Paris: J.-P. Migne, 1854), 957.

23. Jean-Louis Chrétien, *Hand to Hand: Listening to the Work of Art,* trans. Stephen E. Lewis (New York: Fordham University Press, 2003), 1–17.

justice through punishment, but also toward the edification of the one to whom he is speaking. Continuing an image from Chardon, we may say that it is as though Christ knocks his interlocutor off center with his words so that the latter may find his or her center of gravity anew outside of himself or herself.[24]

At the beginning of this chapter, I suggested that Christ's anger should not be viewed as a phenomenon removed from his salvific mission. To wit, I have argued that Jesus' anger is restorative of justice and perfective of the human person in relation to God—in a word, his anger is redemptive *like* the Cross is redemptive. To say that anger is redemptive and the Cross is redemptive is not yet, however, to say that the Cross is an event of anger. Would this be going too far? If anger as redemptive does not apply to the Crucifixion, it is difficult to see that this idea has much traction.

But for a few trace elements in the Gospel narratives, the Crucifixion seems to be marked by everything that we associate with the reception of anger, rather than its origination. Lk 12:49–53, however, seems to mix active expressions of violence with the Passion that Jesus is to endure; these verses speak (in the following order) of fire, baptism, and division.[25]

24. However, does the claim that Jesus' anger is fundamentally therapeutic, even maieutic, not betray a disregard of the obvious fact that not everyone whom Jesus confronted was actually changed for the better? We may give two responses. First, the words of Jesus as they are recorded by the evangelists are not limited to their immediate auditors; thus Christ's anger may not have helped the Pharisees as much as it does someone reading about them. Second, that Jesus' anger did not have an immediate effect in specific cases does not in any way change the purpose and character of his anger. God's overtures, Trent reminds us, are resistible.

25. For the sake of convenience, these verses in the Revised Standard Version are: "[49] I came to cast fire upon the earth; and would that it were already kindled! [50] I have a baptism to be baptized with; and how I am constrained [συνέχ-

We will have to ask firstly whether the baptism that Jesus is to receive is really identifiable with his Passion, secondly whether or not the three themes just mentioned are related, and thirdly, if so, what a relationship between them might mean.

Jesus' "baptism" clearly seems to be a reference to his Passion. The term that Luke uses in v. 50 to describe Jesus' interior state is συνέχομαι. The word συνέχω is employed only once by the other evangelists (in an unrelated context); in contrast, it is used often by Luke. However, the only other scenes in Lk-Acts in which it is used in direct connection to Jesus are a healing story and the Crucifixion.[26] This proves nothing, of course, but it appears more significant when coupled with another word used in v. 50, τελεσθῇ. Luke only uses τελέω four other times and, of these instances, only once does Luke employ the term apart from Jesus' suffering,[27] while it refers three of those times to the completion of his Passion.[28] It is probable that τελεσθῇ in v. 50 likewise signifies the completion of his suffering. It is difficult to imagine what the "baptism" in v. 50 could mean if not Jesus' Passion; a water baptism is ruled out by Lk 3:21 and the text leaves no other clue to the matter into which Jesus is to be immersed.

---

ομαι] until it is accomplished [τελεσθῇ]! [51] Do you think that I have come to give peace on earth? No, I tell you, but rather division [διαμερισμόν]; [52] for henceforth in one house there will be five divided [διαμεμερισμένοι], three against two and two against three; [53] they will be divided [διαμερισθήσονται], father against son and son against father, mother against daughter and daughter against her mother, mother-in-law against her daughter-in-law and daughter-in-law against her mother-in-law." I have quoted this text from Kurt Aland, ed., *Synopsis of the Four Gospels: English Edition* (N.p.: United Bible Societies, 1982), 186. I have spliced in the Greek words that will be at issue in the next paragraphs.

26. Lk 8:45 and 22:63.

27. Lk 2:36.

28. Lk 18:31, 22:37; Acts 13:29.

To begin to formulate an answer to the second question—of whether fire, baptism, and division are related or not—we can point to a possible connection in Luke's mind between baptism and fire in view of Lk 3:16, which explicitly relates baptism by Jesus to fire. Perhaps a similar connection exists in Luke's understanding between division and fire and thus between vv. 49 and 51–53; the same word for "divide" (in the substantive and verbal forms) that is used three times in 12:51–53 (διαμερισμός; διαμερίζω) is also used, together with "fire," in Acts 2:3. It may be that these connections are merely circumstantial and of themselves provide no real evidence that the baptism that Jesus is to receive (instead of give) in 12:50 is qualified by the fire of 12:49 or that the fire and division of 12:49 and 12:51–53 are mutually illuminating. However, if we look at the flow of these verses together, especially the closely parallel structures of vv. 49 and 50, it is difficult to deny that only when these verses are taken together do we have Luke's meaning.

If Jesus' received baptism in v. 50 is embedded not casually but deliberately between fire in v. 49 and division in vv. 51–53, we cannot escape the question of what purpose Luke means such violent, even martial, imagery to serve in connection with this baptism. If vv. 49 and 51–53 stand as chiastic brackets, how do these reflect upon Jesus' intercalated comment on his Passion?

However true it may be that Luke gives a passing and oblique signal of an active aggression at the heart of the Crucifixion, such a theme is not explicit in the Passion narratives themselves. In dark contrast to certain moments during his public ministry, the Passion is the event in which Jesus battles evil in the context of our anger instead of his own, *flagello iracundiae nostrae* (by the whip of our anger). Is there then any way of thinking of the Crucifixion as the culmination of *Christ's* anger rather than that of the infernal anger that has nailed him to the Cross?

In only the simplest of human scenarios is one person *only* the angry one and another person *only* the recipient of anger. To think of the Crucified Christ as simply the recipient of the world's hatred and anger seems to represent an oversimplification that disallows any but an incidental connection between his death and the life that he lived on earth. Moreover, we have to wonder what kind of human psychology such a portrayal would fit. Is there anyone unjustly punished who is not hotly indignant? Can we really suppose that Jesus would have been angry when the Temple was overrun by sellers but not so when the Temple was being destroyed?[29] Instead I think it more reasonable to hold that Jesus' anger, the human fire of divine charity, burned through to the end of his life. The Crucifixion—and, following on this integrally, the Resurrection—are a struggle between two angers, one depraved and the other holy, in which human anger succumbs to the force of its divine challenger.

We must not downplay the passivity of Christ on the Cross; however, we must understand this in the proper perspective.[30] Anger will only be manifested outwardly as a passion (it is always inwardly a passion) where the angry person

29. Cf., e.g., Jn. 2:19–21.

30. The well-known contrast between John's Passion account and those of the Synoptics is relevant here.

knows that this passivity itself is to play a role in the immanent or eventual activity of vindication. One common expression of this truth—to which we cannot limit ourselves in the present case—is the adage "Revenge is a dish best served cold." For Jesus, the passive moment of anger is deeper in significance than a simple biding of his time until the opportune moment to strike, although this characterization has a qualified applicability to resurrection. The verses just mentioned in Lk 12 remind us that Jesus' Passion is purposeful. The Lord understands not just that he will suffer or even only those for whom he will suffer, as central as these truths are to his mission. These two features of his knowledge are of no consequence unless he understands the meaning of this suffering. Yet, the meaning of Christ's suffering is only the meaning that Charity itself actively gives to it in the Resurrection.

We have seen that anger is not incidental to Christ's drive through death toward resurrection. By extension we can see that his emotions in general cannot stand as an afterthought in any complete account of salvation. Although sensitivity is toward the bottom of the classical anthropological taxonomy (intellect, will, affectivity) that we have been tacitly following in this book, it is of capital importance. Signaling the importance of affectivity teaches us to relate to Jesus in his solidarity with us, that is, as having profoundly entered into the human condition. In thinking about this mystery, we may also correctly infer that his affectivity is salvific because it is our affectivity that he saves. Our immediate concern here, however, has been more limited. In underscoring the reality of Jesus' emotional life we have been concerned with the view that this gives us of a Person concentrated on the mission of salvation in a way that is integral of every human reality and faculty. If nature has no superfluity,[31] neither does grace. There is nothing about Jesus that is not in some way salvation.[32] Wrath has played an abounding role in this sparing economy precisely because salvation involves a striving against mortality and sin. It is thus from the ardor of Christ's anger, which hunted evil into the darkness of death, that spring the first rays of Easter Resurrection.

31. Cf. St. Thomas Aquinas, *Quaestiones disputatae de potentia,* 3, 7.

32. See Cardinal Joseph Ratzinger, *Eschatology: Death and Eternal Life,* 2nd ed., trans. Michael Waldstein and Aidan Nichols, O.P. (Washington, D.C.: The Catholic University of America Press, 1988), 205: "In himself he is sheer salvation."

# EPILOGUE

Biblical theologians often remind us that the name "Jesus" means something approximating "God saves." What does it mean to say that a man's name, his very identity in the biblical mind-set, is identified with an action? In describing this action itself, I have not been precise. I have said little about *how* this action is accomplished; it suffices for present purposes to have argued *that* the mission in question here is indissociable from the Person who accomplishes it. This has meant specifying the identity of the agent and, since this agent exists and acts in two natures, indicating something of the "personality" of his humanity. In other words, I have prescinded from the workings of salvation itself—bearing in mind only salvation's most necessary features—in order to train attention on the character of the one who saves. Granting that salvation is for all, granting that it is the fullest and truest act of love, granting that it is truly accomplished through human agency (i.e., it is not a voluntaristic game that God plays), and so on, what figure of Savior should we presuppose?

Without precluding the validity of other perspectives and insights, I have tried to supply an answer to this question principally in terms of Christ as Mediator. In a general sense, of course, mediation implies the affinity of one agent with two realities. In the case of Christ, there is not only an ontological gulf between these two realities, the Creator and the created, but the willful separation caused by sin. To mediate, Christ must enfold within himself not only the opposition of finite and Infinite but also moral opposition, which is of an altogether different sort. Theology has readily seen the value of this notion; by God's holding the cold, finite, and fallen—with which Christ, though sinless, is in solidarity—together with his ardent and infinite love together in the space of one Person, one opposite transforms and repristinates the other. But this affirmation raises another question: How are we really to understand Christ's being—to borrow a phrase put to extensive use by Nicholas of Cusa—the Coincidence of Opposites? Where and how is the finite subsumed to the Infinite?[1] When we recast this question in an old way, the answer at once begins to come into view. Gregory Nazianzus's famous dictum, "That which is not assumed is not healed," compels us to see Jesus' mediation carried out on every stratum of human reality.[2] I have attempted to apply this consideration to Christ's ontological foundation (chapter 4), to his human intellect (chapters 1

1. As we have already seen, we must ascribe the work of subsumption, that is, the work of the Incarnation, to the Trinity. God undivided effects the union of finite and Infinite and, as chapters 1 and 4 have shown, the Word does not exert a proper divine causality with respect to his created nature. The question here, however, concerns the nature assumed.

2. Gregory Nazianzus, *Letter to Cledonius the Priest against Apollinaris* (Letter 101).

and 2), to his will (chapter 3), and to his emotional life (chapter 5). Every level of humanity stands in need of healing and it is only through a conscious, free, and total human response that the Trinity heals.

However, we have already seen in this more than that Christ has become human fully, that is, in every human faculty. As Blondel argues, his becoming human means that in some way he embraces and sustains—and so redeems—the lived human reality of every other individual. To say that Jesus is simply one man among others is to say too little, because on this basis alone we can never account for how his action, death, and so on would have an atoning significance for others, unless we are willing to take refuge in an inexplicable divine fiat. Jesus offers a response that is both totally human (it involves all human faculties) and of human totality (it involves others by an organic, rather than an imputed, solidarity). Essential to this is that Jesus embrace humanity in its existential condition and not merely in the abstract. Fallenness is anti-humanity, as evil is the privation of being, but human beings have made this fallenness their own. Thus, God does not only join himself in the Incarnation to everything that is truly and authentically human in order to redeem. Rather, in complete human reality (intellectual, voluntary, affective, corporeal), he follows the "logical" course of sin and evil all the way to annihilation. Christ does not only enfold within himself humanity in all of its natural and ontological complexity; he also so encompasses humanity in its existential trajectory toward death. Since human reality is both historical and free, nature and movement remain interlocked. For this reason, God Incarnate does not take the What of humanity without its Whither. In the totalizing mediation of Jesus, the full sweep of human reality is transplanted from the dust toward which it seeks to return into the love of God that resurrects from death: "Death is swallowed in victory."[3]

In taking as our point of departure a few basic features of salvation, the modus operandi that we have followed has been one of "reverse engineering" in forming a conception of Jesus. Throughout the preceding chapters, I have sought to avoid a notion of salvation—and, by implication, of the Savior—that is informed by intellectual narrowness or by voluntarism. Parts fit together tightly in any intelligible whole. In truth, Christ does not win graces to which he is not profoundly connected in action (chapter 3), he is not a pawn in a game that he does not really understand (chapter 1), the reality that he redeems is not connected to his understanding as mere external object (chapter 2), his emotional life is not peripheral or even extraneous to his saving (chapter 5), he himself is not unlike the unification that he effects (chapter 4), and so on. Rather than accept the unarticulated but pervasive view that, by simple fiat, God establishes a kind of soteriological obstacle course through which his Son must maneuver (while wearing the blindfold of his humanity), I urge that salvation makes sense. Insisting on this does not compromise the free or mysterious (to us) character of God's action; freedom is not arbitrariness. Only if redemption is a game, which God just so happens to will, is the matter of who is involved one of

3. 1 Cor 15:54.

indifference. Instead, the essential facts of redemption determine how we must understand the Savior. For this reason, we likewise cannot be content with a purportedly pure biblicism that claims to read off the personality of Jesus from select texts in Scripture, as if the broader context of Jesus' mission and the scope of salvation had nothing to do with the picture that we form here.

It is essential, then, to understand the figure of Jesus only in connection with salvation and vice versa. In this sense, the circumspection of St. Thomas on the question of the conditioned or unconditioned predestination of the Incarnation is laudable: we have no basis for conceiving of the Incarnate Word apart from his mission.[4] Yet it is not only the Redeemer and redemption that we must hold together. As we saw in chapter 3, we must continue to unify ideas by seeing the redeemed only in the light of the Redeemer. In being saved, we are truly made part of Christ (St. Augustine's *Totus Christus*), even as he has engaged us at the deepest ontological and existential levels. The Christological lines suggested above lend consistency and support to this notion and help us avoid still other voluntarist implications, such as the conception of justification in forensic terms. We have seen that Christ's mediation between created reality and God is anchored in the depths of the human condition and we should conceive of our holding fast to Christ only in terms of a response to this initiative. But the realization of a total human response to Christ becomes far less plausible where we fail to see Christ—as the

4. See *ST* 3, 1, 3.

condition for this—with the full deployment of his humanity, concentrated in a specific love for us. Love responds to love in kind. The understanding of Jesus' understanding and action that I have outlined here allows us to think of ourselves as present during the events of redemption in the intentions and intentionality of a zealously active Christ, rather than as the beneficiaries of an arranged transfer of merit after the fact.

We must understand the merit of Jesus' Passion in connection with the whole significance of his historical action and human character. Otherwise, we can easily form the simplistic and crudely emptional idea that something—forgiveness, justification, eternal life—is purchased and reserved as a bequest to nameless heirs. Jesus does not merit something for us unless by this that he wins himself, the whole man, back from a fight with death and evil and wins us too, precisely because we were already in him. If we are willing to allow that we were in Jesus on the Cross and walking out of the Tomb, as he perfected virtue for us and angrily fought against the evil within us that threatens us, then we trade a *Deus ludens* for God Saves.

# BIBLIOGRAPHY


Adam, Karl. *The Christ of Faith: The Christology of the Church.* Translated by Joyce Crick. New York: Pantheon Books, 1957.

Aland, Kurt, ed. *Synopsis of the Four Gospels: English Edition.* N.p.: United Bible Societies, 1982.

Alfaro, Juan, S.J. "Person and Grace." In *Man before God: Readings in Theology,* edited by Juan Alfaro and Denis Burkhard, (New York: P. J. Kenedy & Sons, 1966), 174–98.

Amato, Angelo. *Gesù il signore: Saggio di cristologia.* 3rd ed. Bologna: Edizioni Dehoniane Bologna, 1993.

Antonelli, Mario. *L'Eucaristia nell' "Action" (1893) di Blondel: La chiave di volta di un'apologetica filosofica.* Milan: Glossa, 1991.

Aristotle. *Nicomachean Ethics.* Translated by H. Rackham. Edited by E. H. Warmington. The Loeb Classic Library, Aristotle, XIX, 73. Cambridge, Mass., and London: Harvard University Press and William Heinemann, 1934.

Aquinas, Thomas. *Quaestiones disputatae et quaestiones duodecim quodlibetales.* 7th ed. Vol. 2. Rome: Domus Editorialis Marietti Taurini, 1942.

———. *Question disputée l'union du Verbe incarné (De unione Verbi incarnati).* Translated by Marie-Hélène Deloffre. Paris: Librairie Philosophique J. Vrin, 2000.

Augustine. *Confessions.* Translated by Henry Chadwick. New York: Oxford University Press, 1991.

———. "Exposition of Psalm 85." In *The Works of St. Augustine: A Translation for the 21st Century,* 18. Edited by John E. Rotelle, O.S.A., 220–45. New York: New City Press, 2002.

Bainvel, Jean V., S.J. *Devotion to the Sacred Heart: The Doctrine and Its History.* Translated by E. Leahy. 5th ed. London: Burns, Oates and Washbourne, 1924.

von Balthasar, Hans Urs. *Love Alone: The Way of Revelation.* London: Sheed & Ward, 1968.

———. "Nine Theses in Christian Ethics." In *Readings in Moral Theology, No. 2: The Distintiveness of Christian Ethics,* edited by Charles Curran and Richard McCormick, S.J., (New York: Paulist Press, 1980), 190–206.

———. *Spouse of the Word.* Vol. 2, *Explorations in Theology.* San Francisco: Ignatius Press, 1991.

———. *Theo-Drama: Theological Dramatic Theory.* Vol. 3, *Dramatis Personae: Persons in Christ.* Translated by Graham Harrison. San Francisco: Ignatius Press, 1992.

Bathrellos, Demetrios. *The Byzantine Christ: Person, Nature, and Will in the Christology of Saint Maximus the Confessor.* Edited by Gillian Clark and Andrew Louth. Oxford Early Christian Studies. Oxford, U.K.: Oxford University Press, 2004.

Battaglia, Vincenzo, O.F.M. "I 'Sentimenti' del Signore Gesù: Un modello cristologico per la vita spirituale e l'agire morale." *Antonianum* 81 (2006): 209–55.

Bayne, Tim. "The Inclusion Model of the Incarnation: Problems and Prospects." *Religious Studies* 37, no. 2 (2001): 125–41.

Bennett, M. R., and P. M. S. Hacker. *Philosophical Foundations of Neuroscience.* Malden, Mass.: Blackwell, 2003.

Blondel, Maurice. *La Psychologie dramatiqued du mystère de la passion a Oberammergau.* Paris: Librairie Bloud & Cie, 1910.

———. *Carnets Intimes.* Vol. 1 (1883–1894). Paris: Les Éditions du Cerf, 1961.

———. *The Letter on Apologetics and History and Dogma.* Translated by Alexander Dru and Illtyd Trethowan. Grand Rapids, Mich.: William B. Eerdmans, 1964.

———. *Carnets Intimes.* Vol. 2 (1894–1949). Paris: Les Éditions du Cerf, 1966.

———. "Philosophy Fulfilled in Christianity." In *Christian Witness in the Secular City,* edited by Everett J. Morgan, 89–97. Chicago: Loyola University Press, 1970.

———. *L'Action: Essay on a Critique of Life and a Science of Practice (1893).* Translated by Oliva Blanchette. Notre Dame, Ind.: University of Notre Dame Press, 1984.

Blondel, Maurice, and Auguste Valensin. *Correspondance (1899–1912): Maurice Blondel et Auguste Valensin.* 2 vols. Vol. 1, Paris: Aubier, Éditions Montaigne, 1957.

Bosco, Eugenio M., O.Carm. *La scienza umana del Cristo in San Tommaso e San Bonaventura: Divergenze e concordanze.* Naples: "Tipomeccanica" Marra, 1954.

Brown, Raymond E., S.S. *An Introduction to New Testament Christology.* New York and Mahwah, N.J.: Paulist Press, 1994.

Buber, Martin. *Eclipse of God: Studies in the Relation between Religion and Philosophy.* Translated by Norbert Guterman, Maurice Friedman, Eugene Kamenka, and I. M. Lask. New York: Harper & Row, 1957.

———. *I and Thou.* 2nd ed. Translated by Ronald Gregor Smith. New York: Charles Scribner's Sons, 1958.

Cé, Marco. "La Discussione sulla coscienza umana di Cristo nella teologia moderna." *La Scuola Cattolica* 80 (1952): 265–303.

Cessario, Romanus, O.P. "Incarnate Wisdom and the Immediacy of Christ's Salvific Knowledge." In *Atti del IX Congresso tomistico internazionale, 5: Problemi teologici alla luce dell'Aquinate,* edited by Antonio Piolanti, 334–40 (Vatican City: Libreria Editrice Vaticana, 1991).

Chrétien, Jean-Louis. *Le regard de l'amour.* Paris: Desclée de Brouwer, 2000.

———. *Hand to Hand: Listening to the Work of Art.* Translated by Stephen E. Lewis. New York: Fordham University Press, 2003.

Ciappi, Luigi (Aloysius). "De unitate Ontologica ac Psychologica Personae Christi." *Angelicum* 29 (1952): 182–89.

Claudel, Paul. "Le Coeur compte." In *Le Coeur,* edited by Paul Claudel, 11–13. Bruges: Desclée de Brouwer, 1950.

Coffey, David M. "The Theandric Nature of Christ." *Theological Studies* 60 (1999): 405–31.

———. "Quaestio Disputata: Response to Neil Ormerod, and Beyond." *Theological Studies* 68 (2007): 900–915.

de Cointet, Pierre. "Le Médiateur: La Trilogie et La Philosophie et L'Esprit Chrétien." In *Le Christ de Maurice Blondel,* edited by René Virgoulay, 147–86. Paris: Desclée, 2003.

Congar, Yves, O.P. "Pour une Christologie pneumatologique: Note bibliographique." *Revue des sciences philosophiques et théologiques* 63, no. 3 (1979): 435–42.

Corvez, M., O.P. "La 'distinction réelle' et l'unicité de l'être dans le Christ." *Revue Thomiste* 59 (1959): 704–15.

Coutagne, Marie-Jeanne. "Le Christ et l'énigme du monde: La christologie blondélienne 1916–1925." In *Le Christ de Maurice Blondel,* edited by René Virgoulay, 85–114. Paris: Desclée, 2003.

Crowe, Frederick E. "The Mind of Jesus." *Communio* 1, no. 4 (1974): 365–84.

———, ed. *A Third Collection: Papers by Bernard J. F. Lonergan, S.J.* New York, Mahwah, N.J., and London: Paulist Press and Geoffrey Chapman, 1985.

Davidson, Ivor. "'Not My Will but Yours Be Done': The Ontological Dynamics of Incarnational Intention." *International Journal of Systematic Theology* 7, no. 2 (2005): 178–204.

Delhaye, Philippe. "La charité, 'premier commandement' chrétien chez S. Bonaventure." In *S. Bonaventura: 1274–1974,* Vol. 4: *Theologica,* 503–21. Grottaferrata, Italy: Collegio S. Bonaventura, 1974.

———. "La "loi nouvelle" dans l'enseignement de S. Thomas." In *San Tommaso e la filosofia del diritto oggi: Saggi,* edited by Pontificia Accademia Romana di S. Tommaso D'Aquino, 73–103. Rome: Pontificia Accademia Romana di S. Tommaso D'Aquino and Città Nuova Editrice, 1989.

Denzinger, Heinrich, and Adolf Schönmetzer, S.J., eds. *Enchiridion symbolorum: Definitionum et declarationum de rebus fidei et morum.* 36th ed. Barcelona, Spain; Freiburg im Breisgau, Germany; and Rome: Herder, 1976.

Diepen, Herman Michel, O.S.B. *La Théologie de L'Emmanuel: Les Lignes maîtresses d'une Christologie.* Bruges: Desclée de Brouwer, 1960.

Dupuis, Jacques, S.J., and Josef Neuner, S.J., eds. *The Christian Faith in the Doctrinal Documents of the Catholic Church.* 7th ed. New York: Alba House, 2001.

Dupuis, Jacques, S.J. *Who Do You Say I Am? Introduction to Christology.* Maryknoll, N.Y.: Orbis Books, 1994.

Duquoc, Christian. *Christologie: Essai dogmatique.* Paris: Les Éditions du Cerf, 1972.

Durand, Alexandre. "La Science du Christ." *Nouvelle Revue Théologique* 71 (1949): 497–503.

Engelbert Gutwenger, S.J. "The Problem of Christ's Knowledge." In *Who Is Jesus of Nazareth?* New York and Glen Rock, N.J.: Paulist Press, 1965.

Evans, Craig A. "Patristic Interpretation of Mark 2:26: 'When Abiathar Was High Priest.'" *Vigiliae Christianae* 40 (1986): 183–86.

Fascher, Erich. "Von dem Tage aber und von der Stunde weiß niemand ...": Der Anstoß in Mark. 13, 32 (Matth. 24, 36)—Eine exegetische Skizze zum Verhältnis von historisch-kritischer und christologischer Interpretation." In *Ruf und Antwort: Festgabe für Emil Fuchs zum 90. Geburtstag,* 475–83. Leipzig: Koehler & Amelang, 1964.

Gabellieri, Emmanuel. "'Vinculum' et 'sursum': Métaphysique, christologie et ontologie trinitaire ou les 'exigences philosphiques du christianisme'." In *Le Christ de Maurice Blondel,* edited by René Virgoulay, 187–201. Paris: Desclée, 2003.

Galot, Jean, S.J. "La psychologie du Christ." *Nouvelle Revue Théologique* 80, no. 4 (1958): 337–58.

Galtier, Paul. "La conscience humaine du Christ." *Gregorianum* 35, no. 2 (1954): 225–46.

Galvin, John P. "The Death of Jesus in Contemporary Theology: Systematic Perspectives and Historical Issues." *Horizons* 13, no. 2 (1986): 239–52.

———. "From the Humanity of Christ to the Jesus of History: A Paradigm Shift in Catholic Christology." *Theological Studies* 55 (1994): 252–73.

Garrigou-Lagrange, Réginald, O.P. "L'unique personnalité du Christ." *Angelicum* 29 (1952): 60–75.

Geach, Peter. *Providence and Evil: The Stanton Lectures, 1971–1972.* London and New York: Cambridge University Press, 1977.

Glorieux, Palemon. "La révélation du Pére." *Mélanges de science religieuse* 42, no. 1 (1985): 21–41.

Gondreau, Paul. *The Passions of Christ's Soul in the Theology of St. Thomas Aquinas.* Münster, Germany: Aschendorff Verlag GmbH & Co., 2002.

Guillet, Jacques, S.J. *The Consciousness of Jesus.* Translated by Edmond Bonin. New York, Paramus, N.J., and Toronto: Newman Press, 1972.

Gumerlock, Francis X. "Mark 13:32 and Christ's Supposed Ignorance: Four Patristic Solutions." *Trinity Journal* 28, no. 2 (2007): 205–13.

Hastings, Adrian. "Christ's Act of Existence." *Downside Review* 73, no. 232 (1955): 139–59.

Haubst, R. "Welche Ich spricht Christus?" *Trierer theologische Zeitschrift* 66 (1957): 1–20.

Hayes, Zachary, O.F.M. "The Plurality of *Esse* in Christ According to

Matthew of Aquasparta." In *Essays Honoring Allan B. Wolter,* edited by William A. Frank and Girard J. Etzkorn, 153–64. St. Bonaventure, N.Y.: Franciscan Institute of St. Bonaventure University, 1985.

Héris, Charles-Vincent. "A propos de la psychologie humaine du Christ." *Revue Thomiste* 51 (1951): 465–68.

———. "A propos d'un article sur la psychologie du Christ." *Revue des sciences philosophiques et théologiques* 43, no. 3 (1959): 462–71.

———. "Problème de christologie. La conscience de Jésus." *Esprit et Vie* 81 (1971): 672–79.

van Hooff, A. E. "Panchristismus: Bezugspunkt von Blondels l'Action." *Zeitschrift für Katholische Theologie* 109, no. 4 (1987): 416–30.

Houlgate, Stephen. *The Opening of Hegel's Logic: From Being to Infinity.* Edited by Adriann Peperzak et al. Purdue University Press Series in the History of Philosophy. West Lafayette, Ind.: Purdue University Press, 2006.

Jammarrone, Luigi, O.F.M. Conv. *L'Unità psicologica in Cristo.* Edited by Pontificia Facultas Theologica S. Bonaventurae Ordinis Fratrum Minorum Conventualium in Urbe. Selecta Seraphica, 1. Rome: Editrice "Miscellanea Francescana", 1962.

Kereszty, Roch, O. Cist. "Psychological Subject and Consciousness in Christ." *Communio* 11, no. 3 (1984): 258–77.

de Lacey, D. R. "Jesus as Mediator." *Journal for the Study of the New Testament* 29 (1987): 101–21.

Levering, Matthew. *Christ's Fulfillment of Torah and Temple: Salvation According to Thomas Aquinas.* Notre Dame, Ind.: University of Notre Dame Press, 2002.

Latour, Jean-Jacques. "Imago Dei invisibilis: Esquisses sur les relations de l'anthropologie chrétienne et de la psychologie du Christ." In *Problèmes actuels de christologie,* edited by Humbert Bouëssé and Jean-Jacques Latour, 227–64. Bruges: Desclée de Brouwer, 1965.

Le Troquer, René, P.S.S. *What Is Man?* Translated by Eric Earnshaw Smith. Edited by Henri Daniel-Rops. In *Twentieth Century Encyclopedia of Catholicism,* 3:31. New York: Hawthorn Books, 1961.

Léthel, François-Marie. *Théologie de l'agonie du Christ: La liberté humaine du Fils de Dieu et son importance sotériologique mises en lumière par Saint Maxime Confesseur.* Edited by Charles Kannengiesser. Théologie Historique, 52. Paris: Éditions Beauchesne, 1979.

Lonergan, Bernard, S.J. "Christ as Subject: A Reply." In *Collection: Papers by Bernard Lonergan,* edited by F. E. Crowe, S.J., 164–97. New York: Herder & Herder, 1967.

———. *The Ontological and Psychological Constitution of Christ.* Translated by Michael G. Shields. Edited by Michael G. Shields, Frederick E. Crowe, and Robert M. Doran. In *Collected Words of Bernard Lonergan*, vol. 7. Toronto; Buffalo, N.Y.; and London: University of Toronto Press, 2002.

de Lubac, Henri, S.J. "A Meditation on the Principle of the Moral Life." *Communio* 26 (1999): 418–28.

———, ed. *Pierre Teilhard de Chardin, Maurice Blondel: Correspondence.* Translated by William Whitman. New York: Herder & Herder, 1967.

Madigan, Kevin. "*Christus Nesciens*? Was Christ Ignorant of the Day of Judgment? Arian and Orthodox Interpretations of Mark 13:32 in the Ancient Latin West." *Harvard Theological Review* 96, no. 3 (2003): 255–78.

Malevez, Léopold, S.J. "L'Église dans le Christ, II." *Recherches de Science religieuse* 25 (1935): 418–40.

Malloy, Christopher J. *Engrafted into Christ: A Critique of the Joint Declaration.* American University Studies, Series 71, Theology and Religion, Vol. 233. New York: Peter Lang, 2005.

Maloney, Raymond, S.J. *The Knowledge of Christ: Problems in Theology.* London and New York: Continuum, 1999.

———. "The Mind of Christ in Transcendental Theology: Rahner, Lonergan and Crowe." *Heythrop Journal* 25 (1984): 288–300.

Mansini, Guy, O.S.B. "Understanding St. Thomas on Christ's Immediate Knowledge of God." *The Thomist* 59, no. 1 (1995): 91–124.

Maritain, Jacques. *On the Grace and Humanity of Jesus.* New York: Herder & Herder, 1969.

Marlé, René, S.J. *Au coeur de la crise moderniste: Le dossier inédit d'une controverse.* Paris: Aubier, Éditions Montaigne, 1960.

McDermott, John, S.J. *Love and Understanding: The Relation of Will and Intellect in Pierre Rousselot's Christological Vision.* Analecta Gregoriana, 229, B, 77. Rome: Università Gregoriana Editrice, 1983.

———. "The Christologies of Karl Rahner, II." *Gregorianum* 67, no. 2 (1986): 297–327.

———. "How Did Jesus Know He Was God? The Ontological Psychology of Mark 10:17–22." *Irish Theological Quarterly* 74, no. 3 (2009): 272–97.

McTaggart, John McTaggart Ellis. *A Commentary on Hegel's Logic.* New York: Russell & Russell, 1964.

Mongeau, Gilles, S.J. "The Human and Divine Knowing of the Incarnate Word." *Josephinum Journal of Theology* 12 (2005): 30–42.

Most, William G. *The Consciousness of Christ.* Front Royal, Va.: Christendom Publications, 1980.

Mouroux, Jean. "Maurice Blondel et la conscience du Christ." In *L'Homme devant Dieu: Mélanges offerts au Père Henri de Lubac,* 185–207. Paris: Aubier, 1964.

Pannenberg, Wolfhart. *Jesus—God and Man.* 2nd ed. Translated by Lewis L. Wilkins and Duane A. Priebe. Philadelphia: Westminster Press, 1977.

Patfoort, Albert. "L'enseignement de saint Thomas sur l''esse' du Christ." In *Problèmes actuels de christologie,* ed. Humbert Bouëssé and Jean-Jacques Latour, 101–28. Paris: Desclée de Brouwer, 1965.

Perego, Angelo, S.J. "Sull'Unità psicologica di Cristo: In margine ad un notevole studio recente." *Ephemerides Carmeliticae* 12 (1961): 105–15.

Périco, Yvette. "De la foi au Christ à la Christologie philosophique." In *Le Christ de Maurice Blondel,* ed. René Virgoulay, 11–34. Paris: Desclée, 2003.

Petrus Chrysologus [Peter Chrysologus]. *Sermo XXXII: De eo qui habebat manum aridam in Opera Omnia in Patrologiae cursus completus.* Patrologia Latina, Vol. 52. Volume edited by Sebastianus Pauli. Series edited by J.-P.Migne. Paris: J.-P. Migne, 1846.

Philippe de la Trinité. "A propos de la conscience du Christ: Une faux problème théologique." *Ephemerides Carmeliticae* 11 (1960): 3–52.

Piolanti, Antonio. "L'Essere del Verbo Incarnato." *Divinitas* 3 (1959): 77–94.

Pius XII. "Sempiternus Rex: Encyclical Letter of Pope Pius XII on the Fifteenth Centenary of the Council of Chalcedon." In *Collected Encyclicals of His Holiness Pope Pius XII, 1939–1954,* edited by the National Catholic Welfare Conference, 1–20 (Washington, D.C.: Ransdell, 1954).

Rahner, Karl, S.J. "Dogmatic Reflections on the Knowledge and Self-Consciousness of Christ." In *Theological Investigations,* 5: 193–215. Baltimore: Helicon Press, 1966.

———. "'Behold This Heart!': Preliminaries to a Theology of Devotion to the Sacred Heart." In *Theological Investigations,* edited by Karl Rahner, S.J., 3: 321–30. Baltimore and London: Helicon Press and Darton, Longman & Todd, 1967.

———. "Some Theses for a Theology of Devotion to the Sacred Heart." In *Theological Investigations,* edited by Karl Rahner, S.J., 3: 331–52. Baltimore and London: Helicon Press and Darton, Longman & Todd, 1967.

———. "The Body in the Order of Salvation." In *Theological Investigations,* 17: 71–89. New York: Crossroad, 1981.

Ratzinger, Cardinal Joseph. *Eschatology: Death and Eternal Life.* 2nd ed. Translated by Michael Waldstein and Aidan Nichols, O.P. Washington, D.C.: The Catholic University of America Press, 1988.

Riedlinger, Helmut. *Geschichtlichkeit und Vollendung des Wissens Christi. Quaestiones Disputatae,* 32. Edited by Karl Rahner and Heinrich Schlier. Freiburg, Basel, and Vienna: Herder, 1966.

Rosenberg, Randall S. "Christ's Human Knowledge: A Conversation with Lonergan and Balthasar." *Theological Studies* 71 (2010): 817–45.

Rupertus Abbas Tuitiensis [Rupert of Deutz]. *Commentaria in Apocalypsim Joannis Apostoli in Patrologiae cursus completus.* Patrologia Latina, Vol. 169. Edited by J.-P. Migne. Paris: J.-P. Migne, 1854.

Sarassin, Claude. *Plein de grâce et de vérité: Théologie de l'âme du Christ selon Saint Thomas d'Aquin.* Venasque, France: Éditions du Carmel, 1992.

Schoot, Henk J. M. "The Ineffable Being of Christ According to Thomas Aquinas." In *Atti del IX Congresso tomistico internazionale, 5: Problemi teologici alla luce dell'Aquinate,* edited by Antonio Piolanti, 273–84 (Vatican City: Libreria Editrice Vaticana, 1991).

Schweitzer, Albert. *The Quest of the Historical Jesus: A Critical Study of Its Progress from Reimarus to Wrede.* Translated by W. Montgomery. New York: Macmillan, 1948.

Scotus, John Duns. *Opera Omnia,* Vol. 20, *Lectura in Librum Tertium Sententiarum.* Edited by Commissio Scotistica. Vatican City: Typis Vaticanis, 1950.

Spaccapelo, Natalino, S.J. "La coscienza di Cristo." *Science et Esprit* 26, no. 1 (1974): 5–37.

Stierli, Josef, ed. *Heart of the Saviour.* Freiburg: Herder & Herder, 1957.

Sullivan, J. W. "Matter for Heaven: Blondel, Christ, and Creation." *Ephemerides Theologicae Lovanienses* 64, no. 1 (1988): 60–83.

Tanner, Norman, S.J., ed. *Decrees of the Ecumenical Councils,* Vol. 2, *Trent to Vatican II.* London and Washington, D.C.: Sheed & Ward and Georgetown University Press, 1990.

Tekippe, Terry J. "Towards a Systematic Understanding of the Vision in Christ." *Method: Journal of Lonergan Studies* 11 (1993): 77–101.

Theobald, Christoph. "La Christologie transcendentale dans 'L'Action' (1893) de Maurice Blondel." *Recherches de Science religieuse* 81, no. 3 (1993): 421–58.

Tilliette, Xavier. "Maurice Blondel et la controverse christologique." In

*Le Modernisme,* edited by Pierre Colin and Dominique Dubarle, 129–60. Paris: Editions Beauchesne, 1980.

———. "Is a Philosophical Christology Possible?" In *Problems and Perspectives of Fundamental Theology,* edited by René Latourelle and Gerald O'Collins, 135–50. New York: Paulist Press, 1982.

———. "Le panchristisme dans L'Action et les premiers écrits." In *Le Christ de Maurice Blondel,* edited by René Virgoulay, 35–57. Paris: Desclée, 2003.

Torrell, Jean-Pierre. "S. Thomas d'Aquin et la science du Christ: Une relecture des questions 9–12 de la "Tertia Pars" de la Somme de Théologie." In *Saint Thomas au XXe siècle: Colloque du centenaire de la "Revue thomiste" (1893–1992), Toulouse, 25–28 mars 1993,* edited by Serge-Thomas Bonino, O.P., 394–409. Paris: Éditions Saint-Paul, 1994.

Virgoulay, René. "Exégèse, théologie et philosophie dans la réflexion christologique." *Recherches de Science religieuse* 88, no. 4 (2000): 561–78.

———. "La christologie blondélienne dans la crise moderniste." In *Le Christ de Maurice Blondel,* edited by René Virgoulay, 59–84. Paris: Desclée, 2003.

———. "Postface." In *Le Christ de Maurice Blondel,* edited by René Virgoulay, 203–8 (Paris: Desclée, 2003).

Vögtle, Anton. "Exegetische Erwägungen über das Wissen und Selbstbewusstsein Jesu." In *Gott in Welt: Festgabe für Karl Rahner,* ed. Herbert Vorgrimler, 1: 608–55. Freiburg im Breisgau, Basel, and Vienna: Verlag Herder KG, 1964.

Warfield, Benjamin Breckinridge. *The Person and Work of Christ.* Edited by Samuel G. Craig. Philadelphia: The Presbyterian and Reformed Publishing Company, 1950.

Weber, Jeanne, O.S.B. "Devotion to the Sacred Heart: History, Theology, and Liturgical Celebration." *Worship* 72, no. 3 (1998): 236–54.

Weinandy, Thomas G., O.F.M., Cap. "The Human 'I' of Jesus." *Irish Theological Quarterly* 62, no. 4 (1996): 259–68.

———. "Jesus' Filial Vision of the Father." *Pro Ecclesia* 13, no. 2 (2004): 189–201.

White, Thomas Joseph, O.P. "The Voluntary Action of the Earthly Christ and the Necessity of the Beatific Vision." *The Thomist* 69 (2005): 497–534.

Wilhelmsen, Frederick D. *The Metaphysics of Love.* New York: Sheed & Ward, 1962.

# INDEX

*Jesus the Mediator* was designed in Garamond Premier Pro and typeset by Kachergis Book Design of Pittsboro, North Carolina. It was printed on 60-pound Natures Book Natural and bound by Thomson-Shore of Dexter, Michigan.